I0083561

PHILOSOPHICAL DEBATES

PHILOSOPHICAL DEBATES

Steven M. Cahn

RESOURCE *Publications* • Eugene, Oregon

PHILOSOPHICAL DEBATES

Copyright © 2021 Steven M. Cahn. All rights reserved. Except for brief quotations in critical publications or reviews, no part of this book may be reproduced in any manner without prior written permission from the publisher. Write: Permissions, Wipf and Stock Publishers, 199 W. 8th Ave., Suite 3, Eugene, OR 97401.

Resource Publications
An Imprint of Wipf and Stock Publishers
199 W. 8th Ave., Suite 3
Eugene, OR 97401

www.wipfandstock.com

PAPERBACK ISBN: 978-1-7252-9347-2
HARDCOVER ISBN: 978-1-7252-9348-9
EBOOK ISBN: 978-1-7252-9349-6

04/28/21

To my wife,
Marilyn Ross, M. D.

Contents

Preface

THIS VOLUME COMPLETES A trilogy published by Wipf and Stock that contains my shorter writings. The first volume, *The Road Traveled and Other Essays (2019)*, focuses on my most recent work. The second, *A Philosopher's Journey: Essays from Six Decades* (2020), contains philosophical articles from the 1960s to the present. This third volume, *Philosophical Debates* (2021), includes pieces that comment on the work of others, and I have included edited versions of the material to which I am responding.

Note that some of the selections were written when the custom was to use the noun "man" and the pronoun "he" to refer to all persons regardless of gender, and I have retained the authors' original wording.

I am grateful to the team at Wipf and Stock for their support over many years. Working with them has been a pleasure.

Finally, let me again express my thanks to my brother, Victor L. Cahn, professor emeritus of English at Skidmore College, for his invaluable guidance, and to my wife, Marilyn Ross, M.D., for more than I would try to express in words.

PART I

FATALISM

Introduction

In 1962 RICHARD TAYLOR, who then held a chair in philosophy at Brown University, published an article in the prestigious journal *The Philosophical Review* that astonished its readership. This short, lucid essay with nary a footnote was titled "Fatalism," and in it Taylor argued that when suitably connected, six presuppositions widely accepted by contemporary philosophers implied the fatalistic conclusion that we have no more control over future events than we have now over past ones.

Soon after the article appeared, a spate of criticisms were offered, all maintaining that Taylor's argument was unsound but disagreeing as to what mistake he has supposedly made.[1] As a first-year doctoral student of Taylor's at Columbia University, where he had moved, I wrote a paper for a course I was taking with him developing an extended reply to his critics. With his encouragement, a version of the paper was published in *The Journal of Philosophy*,[2] then became part of my dissertation and served as a chapter in my first book, *Fate, Logic, and Time*.[3]

1. A convenient collection of the responses to Taylor's essay can be found in Steven M. Cahn and Maureen Eckert, eds. *Fate, Time, and Language: An Essay on Free Will by David Foster Wallace* (New York: Columbia University Press, 2011).

2. Steven Cahn, "Fatalistic Arguments," *The Journal of Philosophy,* vol. 61, no. 10, , 295-305.

3. Steven M. Cahn, *Fate, Logic, and Time* (New Haven, CT: Yale University Press, 1967; Eugene, OR: Wipf and Stock Publishers. 2004).

PART I: FATALISM

What is fatalism? It is the doctrine that logic alone implies that people are never free to do other than what they actually do. Note that fatalism makes no reference to the deterministic principle that every event has a cause. Indeed, many determinists believe universal causation is compatible with human freedom. All fatalists, on the other hand, deny free will.[4]

But can fatalism be supported by a philosophically sophisticated argument? Richard Taylor's article meets that challenge and is our first selection. Then, as an example of the writings of his critics, I have included an attempt at refuting his argument offered by John Turk Saunders, at that time a professor at San Fernando Valley State College. What follows are Taylor's response to Saunders, Saunders's answer to Taylor, and my reply to Saunders.

Finally, one clarification. Taylor was not a fatalist, nor am I. We believed, though, that most philosophers subscribe to beliefs that have fatalistic implications.

In particular, consider the assertion that a specific naval commander will order a battle tomorrow. If stated today, is that claim true or, if not true, then false? The majority of philosophers believe truth is timeless, that the time at which a statement is made is irrelevant to its truth. Taylor disagreed. His strategy was to assume that truth is timeless, that is, that the mere passage of time does not enhance or decrease an agent's powers or abilities. Then he drew out what he took to be the unacceptable consequences of that view, thereby seeking to demonstrate its falsity.

4. For other misunderstandings of fatalism, see "Misinterpreting Fatalism" in *A Philosopher's Journey: Essays from Six Decades*, the second volume of this trilogy.

1

Fatalism

RICHARD TAYLOR

A FATALIST—IF THERE IS any such—thinks he cannot do anything about the future. He thinks it is not up to him what is going to happen next year, tomorrow, or the very next moment. He thinks that even his own behavior is not in the least within his power, any more than the motions of the heavenly bodies, the events of remote history, or the political developments in China. It would, accordingly, be pointless for him to deliberate about what he is going to do, for a man deliberates only about such things as he believes are within his power to do and to forego, or to affect by his doings and foregoings.

A fatalist, in short, thinks of the future in the manner in which we all think of the past. For we do all believe that it is not up to us what happened last year, yesterday, or even a moment ago, that these things are not within our power, any more than are the motions of the heavens, the events of remote history or of China. And we are not, in fact, ever tempted to deliberate about what we have done and left undone. At best we can speculate about these things, rejoice over them or repent, draw conclusions from such evidence as we have, or perhaps—if we are not fatalists about the future—extract lessons and precepts to apply henceforth. As for what has in fact happened, we must simply take it as given; the possibilities for action, if there are any, do not lie there. We may, indeed, say that some of those past things *were* once within our power, while they were still future—but this expresses our attitude toward the future, not the past.

There are various ways in which a man might get to thinking in this fatalistic way about the future, but they would be most likely to result from ideas derived from theology or physics. Thus, if God is really all-knowing and all-powerful, then, one might suppose, perhaps he has already arranged for everything to happen just as it is going to happen, and there is nothing left for you or me to do about it. Or, without bringing God into the picture, one might suppose that everything happens in accordance with invariable laws, that whatever happens in the world at any future time is the only thing that can then happen, given that certain other things were happening just before, and that these, in turn, are the only things that can happen at that time, given the total state of the world just before then, and so on, so that again, there is nothing left for us to do about it. True, what we do in the meantime will be a factor in determining how some things finally turn out—but these things that we are *going* to do will perhaps be only the causal consequences of what will be going on just before we do them, and so on back to a not distant point at which it seems obvious that we have nothing to do with what happens then. Many philosophers, particularly in the seventeenth and eighteenth centuries, have found this line of thought quite compelling.

I want to show that certain presuppositions made almost universally in contemporary philosophy yield a proof that fatalism is true, without any recourse to theology or physics. If, to be sure, it is assumed that there is an omniscient god, then that assumption can be worked into the argument so as to convey the reasoning more easily to the unphilosophical imagination, but this assumption would add nothing to the force of the argument, and will therefore be omitted here. And similarly, certain views about natural laws could be appended to the argument, perhaps for similar purposes, but they, too, would add nothing to its validity, and will therefore be ignored.

Presuppositions. The only presuppositions we shall need are the six following.

First, we presuppose that any proposition whatever is either true or, if not true, then false. This is simply the standard interpretation. . .of the law of excluded middle,. . .which is generally admitted to be a necessary truth.

Second, we presuppose that, if any state of affairs is sufficient for, though logically unrelated to, the occurrence of some further condition at the same or any other time, then the former cannot occur without the latter occurring also. This is simply the standard manner in which the concept of *sufficiency* is explicated. Another and perhaps better way of saying the same thing is that, if one state of affairs *ensures* without logically entailing the occurrence of another, then the former cannot occur without the latter occurring. Ingestion of cyanide, for instance, *ensures* death under certain familiar circumstances, though the two states of affairs are not logically related.

Third, we presuppose that, if the occurrence of any condition is necessary for, but logically unrelated to, the occurrence of some other condition at the same or any other time, then the latter cannot occur without the former occurring also. This is simply the standard manner in which the concept of a *necessary* condition is explicated. Another and perhaps better way of saying the same thing is that, if one state of affairs is *essential* for another, then the latter cannot occur without it. Oxygen, for instance, is *essential* to (though it does not by itself ensure) the maintenance of human life—though it is not logically impossible that we should live without it.

Fourth, we presuppose that, if one condition or set of conditions is sufficient for (ensures) another, then that other is necessary (essential) for it, and conversely, if one condition or set of conditions is necessary (essential) for another, then that other is sufficient for (ensures) it. This is but a logical consequence of the second and third presuppositions.

Fifth, we presuppose that no agent can perform any given act if there is lacking, at the same time or any other time, some condition necessary for the occurrence of that act. This follows simply from the idea of anything being essential for the accomplishment of something else. I cannot, for example, live without oxygen, or swim five miles without ever having been in water, or read a given page of print without having learned Russian, or win a certain election without having been nominated, and so on.

And *sixth*, we presuppose that time is not by itself "efficacious"; that is, that the mere passage of time does not augment or diminish the capacities of anything and, in particular, that it does not enhance or decrease an agent's powers or abilities. This means that if any substance or agent gains or loses powers or abilities over the course of time—such as, for instance, the power of a substance to corrode, or a man to do thirty push-ups, and so on—then such gain or loss is always the result of something other than the mere passage of time.

With these presuppositions before us, we now consider two situations in turn, the relations involved in each of them being identical except for certain temporal ones.

The first situation. We imagine that I am about to open my morning newspaper to glance over the headlines. We assume, further, that conditions are such that only if there was a naval battle yesterday does the newspaper carry a certain kind (shape) of headline—i.e., that such a battle is essential for this kind of headline—whereas if it carries a certain different sort (shape) of headline, this will ensure that there was no such battle. Now, then, I am about to perform one or the other of two acts, namely, one of seeing a headline of the first kind, or one of seeing a headline of the second kind. Call these alternative acts S and S' respectively. And call the propositions, "A naval battle occurred yesterday" and "No naval battle occurred yesterday," P and P' respectively. We can assert, then, that if I perform act S, then my doing such will ensure that there was a naval battle yesterday (i.e., that P is true), whereas if I perform S', then my doing that will ensure that no such battle occurred (or, that P' is true).

With reference to this situation, then, let us now ask whether it is up t me which sort of headline I shall read as I open the newspaper; that is, let us see whether the following proposition is true:

(A) It is within my power to do S, and it is also within my power to do S'.

It seems quite obvious that this is not true. For if both these acts were equally within my power, that is, if it were up to me which one to do, then it would also be up to me whether or not a naval battle has taken place, giving me a power over the past which I plainly do not possess. It will be well, however, to express this point in the form of a proof, as follows:

1. If P is true, then it is not within my power to do S' (for in case P is true, then there is, or was, lacking a condition essential for my doing S', the condition, namely, of there being no naval battle yesterday)

2. But if P' is true, then it is not within my power to do S (for a similar reason).

3. But either P is true, or P' is true.

4. Therefore, either it is not within my power to do S, or it is not within my power to do S'; and (A) is accordingly false. A common-sense way of expressing this is to say that what sort of headline I see depends, among other things, on whether a naval battle took place yesterday, and that, in turn, is not up to me.

Now this conclusion is perfectly in accordance with common sense, for we all are, as noted, fatalists with respect to the past. No one considers past events as being within his power to control; we simply have to take them as they have happened and make the best of them. It is significant to note, however, that in the hypothetical sense in which statements of human power or ability are usually formulated, one *does* have power over the past. For we can surely assert that, *if* I do S, this will ensure that a naval battle occurred yesterday, whereas *if*, alternatively, I do S', this will equally ensure the nonoccurrence of such a battle, since these acts are, in terms of our example, quite sufficient for the truth of P and P' respectively. Or we can equally say that I can ensure the occurrence of such a battle yesterday simply by doing S and that I can ensure its nonoccurrence simply by doing S'. Indeed, if I should ask *how* I can go about ensuring that no naval battle occurred yesterday, perfectly straightforward instructions can be given, namely, the instruction to do S' and by all means to avoid doing S. But, of course, the hitch is that I cannot do S' *unless* P' is true, the occurrence of the battle in question rendering me quite powerless to do it.

The second situation. Let us now imagine that I am a naval commander, about to issue my order of the day to the fleet. We assume, further, that, within the totality of other conditions prevailing, my issuing of a certain kind of order will ensure that a naval battle will occur tomorrow, whereas if I issue another kind of order, this will ensure that no naval battle occurs. Now, then, I am about to perform one or the other of these two acts, namely, one of issuing an order of the first sort or one of the second sort. Call these alternative acts O and O' respectively. And call the two propositions, "A naval battle will occur tomorrow" and "No naval battle will occur tomorrow," Q and Q' respectively. We can assert, then, that if I do act O, then my doing such will ensure that there will be a naval battle, whereas if I do O', my doing that will ensure that no naval battle will occur.

With reference to this situation, then, let us now ask whether it is up to me which sort of order I issue; that is, let us see whether the following proposition is true:

(B) It is within my power to do O, and it is also within my power to do O'.

Anyone, except a fatalist, would be inclined to say that, in the situation we have envisaged, this proposition might well be true, that is, that both acts are quite within my power (granting that I cannot do both at once). For in the circumstances we assume to prevail, it is, one would think, up to me as the commander whether the naval battle occurs or not; it depends only on what kind of order I issue, given all the other conditions as they are, and what kind of order is issued is something quite within my power. It is precisely the denial that such propositions are ever true that would render one a fatalist.

But we have, unfortunately, the same formal argument to show that (B) is false that we had for proving the falsity of (A), namely:

1. If Q is true, then it is not within my power to do O' (for in case Q is true, then there is, or will be, lacking a condition essential for my doing O', the condition, namely, of there being no naval battle tomorrow.)

2. But if Q' is true, then it is not within my power to do O (for a similar reason).

3. But either Q is true or Q' is true.

4. Therefore, either it is not within my power to do O, or it is not within my power to do O';

and (B) is accordingly false. Another way of expressing this is to say that what sort of order I issue depends, among other things, on whether a naval battle takes place tomorrow—for in this situation a naval battle tomorrow is (by our fourth presupposition) a necessary condition of my doing O, whereas no naval battle tomorrow is equally essential for my doing O'.

Considerations of time. Here it might be tempting, at first, to say that *time* makes a difference, and that no condition can be necessary for any other *before* that condition exists. But this escape is closed by both our fifth and sixth presuppositions. Surely if some condition, at *any* given time, whether past, present or future, is necessary for the occurrence of something else, and that condition does not in fact exist *at the time it is needed,* then nothing we can do can be of any avail in bringing about that occurrence for which it is necessary. To deny this would be equivalent to saying that I can do something now which is, together with other conditions prevailing, sufficient for, or which ensures, the occurrence of something else in the future, *without* getting that future occurrence as a result.

This is absurd in itself and contrary to our second presupposition. And if one should suggest, in spite of all this, that a state of affairs that exists *not yet* cannot, just because of this temporal removal, be a necessary condition of *anything* existing prior to it, this would be logically equivalent to saying that no present state of affairs can ensure another subsequent to it. We could with equal justice say that a state of affairs, such as yesterday's naval battle, which exists *no longer,* cannot be a necessary condition of anything existing subsequently, there being the same temporal interval here; and this would be arbitrary and false. All that is needed, to restrict the powers that I imagine myself to have to do this or that, is that some condition essential to my doing it *does* not, *did* not, or *will* not occur.

Nor can we wriggle out of fatalism by representing this sort of situation as one in which there is a simple loss of ability or power resulting from the passage of time. For according to our sixth presupposition, the mere passage of time does not enhance or diminish the powers or abilities of anything. We cannot, therefore, say that I have the power to do O' until, say, tomorrow's naval battle occurs, or the power to do O until tomorrow arrives and we find no naval battle occurring, and so on. What restricts the range of my power to do this thing or that is not the mere *temporal* relations between my acts and certain other states of affairs, but the very existence of those states of affairs themselves; and according to our first presupposition, the fact of tomorrow's containing, or lacking, a naval battle, as the case may be, is no less a fact than yesterday's containing or lacking one. If, at any time, I lack the power to perform a certain act, then it can only be the result of something, other than the passage of time, that has happened, is happening, or will happen. The fact that there is *going* to be a naval battle tomorrow is quite enough to render me unable to do O', just as the fact that there *has been* a naval battle yesterday renders me unable to do S', the nonoccurrence of those conditions being essential, respectively, for my doing those things.

Causation. Again, it does no good here to appeal to any particular analyses of causation, or to the fact, if it is one, that causes only "work" forwards and not backwards, for our problem has been formulated without any reference to causation. It may be, for all we know, that causal relations have an unalterable direction (which is an unclear claim in itself), but it is very certain that the relation of necessity and sufficiency between events or states of affairs have not, and it is in terms of these that our data have been described.

The law of excluded middle. There is, of course, one other way to avoid fatalism, and that is to deny the standard interpretation. . .of what is called the law of excluded middle. . ..

Aristotle, according to an interpretation that is sometimes rendered of his *De Interpretatione,* rejected it. According to this view, the disjunction. . .[Q or Q'], which is an instance of the law in question, is a necessary truth. Neither of its disjuncts, however— i.e. neither Q nor Q'—is a necessary truth, nor, indeed, even a truth, but is instead a mere "possibility" or "contingency" (whatever that may mean). And, there is, it would seem, no obvious absurdity in supposing that two propositions, neither of them true and neither of them false, but each "possible," might nevertheless combine into a disjunction which is a necessary truth—for that disjunction might, as this one plainly does, exhaust the possibilities. . ..

We would not, furthermore, be obliged by this line of thought to reject the traditional interpretation of the so-called law of contradiction, which can be expressed by saying that, concerning any proposition, not both it and its contradictory can be true—which is clearly consistent with what is here suggested.

Nor need we suppose that, from a sense of neatness and consistency, we ought to apply the same considerations to our first situation and to proposition (A)—that, if we interpret the law in question as to avoid fatalism with respect to the future, then we ought to retain the same interpretation as it applies to things past. The difference here is that we have not the slightest inclination to suppose that it is at all within our power what happened in the past, or that propositions like (A) in situations such as we have described are ever true, whereas we do, if we are not fatalists, believe that it is sometimes within our power what happens in the future, that is, that propositions like (B) are sometimes true. . ..

PART I: FATALISM

Temporal efficacy. It now becomes apparent, however, that if we seek to avoid fatalism by this device, then we shall have to reject not only our first but also our sixth presupposition; for on this view time will by itself have the power to render true or false certain propositions which were hitherto neither, and this is an "efficacy" or sorts. In fact, it is doubtful whether one can in any way avoid fatalism with respect to the future while conceding that things past are, by virtue of their pastness alone, no longer within our power without also conceding an efficacy to time; for *any* such view will entail that future possibilities, at one time within our power to realize or not, cease to be such *merely* as a result of the passage of time—which is precisely what our sixth presupposition denies. Indeed, this is probably the whole point in casting doubt upon the law of excluded middle in the first place, namely, to call attention to the status of some future things as mere possibilities, thus denying both their complete factuality and their complete lack of it. If so, then our first and sixth presuppositions are inseparably linked, standing or falling together.

The assertion of fatalism. Of course one other possibility remains, and that is to assert, out of a respect for the law of excluded middle and a preference for seeing things under the aspect of eternity, that fatalism is indeed a true doctrine, that propositions such as (B) are, like (A), never true in such situations as we have described, and that the difference in our *attitudes* toward things future and past, which leads us to call some of the former but none of the latter "possibilities," results entirely from epistemological and psychological considerations—such as, that we happen to *know* more about what the past contains than about what is contained in the future, that our memory extends to past experiences rather than future ones, and so on. Apart from subjective feelings of our own power to control things, there seem to be no good philosophical reasons against this opinion, and very strong ones in its favor.

2

Professor Taylor on Fatalism

JOHN TURK SAUNDERS

IN A RECENT ARTICLE Richard Taylor presents us with a problem the solution to which, he suggests, requires either the acceptance of fatalism or the rejection of the traditional interpretation of the logical law of excluded middle. I wish to point out that the problem is solved when one notices an error in Taylor's reasoning, and that once this error is uncovered it is clear that no reason has been provided on behalf of either fatalism or a reinterpretation of the law of excluded middle. . ..

Taylor errs. . .in supposing that no agent has within his power an act for which a necessary condition is lacking. . ..

My knocking upon a thin wooden door with my fist is a sufficient condition for the door's shaking. Hence the door's shaking is a necessary condition for my knocking upon the door. But the door's shaking is not a necessary condition for my *ability* to to knock upon the door. (If it were, then my mere ability to knock upon the door would suffice to make it shake.) I may decide not to knock and the door may not shake, but it does not follow that I did not have it within my power to knock. On the other hand, my having a certain muscle structure is a necessary condition for my ability to knock upon the door. E.g., if my tissues were damaged in certain ways, I could not knock. Suppose that my tissues are damaged in one of these ways. Then I do lack the ability to knock upon the door, since a necessary condition of that ability is lacking. . .. Thus, while a necessary condition for an ability to do something is always a necessary condition for doing it,. . . [o]ften a necessary condition for an act is not a necessary condition for our having the power to perform that act. To suppose otherwise is to adopt a position which logically implies that our mere abilities are sufficient conditions of everything which our acts suffice to produce. In that case we need only possess or acquire the *ability* to perform it, e.g. to work up a sweat I need not exercise. I have only to possess or acquire the ability to exercise.

Now we may solve (or dissolve) Taylor's problem by noting that he is not entitled to conclude: Either is it not within my power to issue order O, or it is not within my power to issue order O'. The occurrence of a naval battle on the morrow is a necessary condition of O but not of the ability to issue O; and the non-occurrence of a naval battle on the morrow is a necessary condition of O' but not of the ability to issue O'. (To suppose otherwise, as Taylor does, is to adopt a position which logically implies that my *ability* to issue order O is a sufficient condition for a naval battle on the morrow and that my *ability* to issue O' is a sufficient condition for the non-occurrence of a naval battle on the morrow.) Thus fades the specter of Taylor's fatalism, leaving in tranquility the law of the excluded middle.

3

Fatalism and Ability

RICHARD TAYLOR

. . .THE THING AT ISSUE is my presupposition that no agent can perform any given act in the absence of some condition necessary for its accomplishment. Saunders says this means only that it is impossible, as a matter of logic, *both* that an agent should perform a certain act y, *and* that there should be lacking some condition, x, necessary for doing y. It does not follow that he is *unable* to do y, but only that he *does not do* y—which is consistent with his having the ability to do y.

Now this is true in the usual sense of ability, which consists in having the skill, strength, equipment, or knowing how. But to make that point is really to miss the point. If there is lacking some condition, x, which is necessary for my doing y, or which is such that y cannot occur without it, then not only do I not do y, I cannot do it, no matter what my natural or acquired abilities might be. This is very obvious when one considers necessary conditions which are lacking in the past. It is less obvious when one considers necessary conditions which are lacking in the future, as Saunders does.

For example, if conditions are such that a naval battle yesterday is a necessary condition for my reading a certain kind of headline today, then, given that no such battle occurred, we can conclude not only that I *do* not read such a headline, but that I *cannot,* that it is not within my power. This is consistent with my knowing how to read it, having the requisite skill and vision, and so on, and thus being able in *that* sense. But if it were in my power to read such a headline, then it logically follows that it would be within my power to make a naval battle occur yesterday, which, we are supposing, did not occur; and this is absurd.

No one doubts that fatalism with respect to the past is true, i.e. that we have no power to make happen what did not in fact happen. My argument showed that we have the same reasons for saying it is true with respect to the future, given the usual interpretation of the law of excluded middle. One does not answer the argument by simply assuming that it is not true with respect to the future.

The issue now turns on the notion of ability. Saunders says that one often has the ability to do something, y, even though there is lacking some condition, x, necessary for its accomplishment. This is true, in the sense of ability that involves skill, strength, requisite organs, or knowing how, which is, admittedly, the ordinary sense. But note that, if we press this sense, then we need no longer be fatalists about the past, for we will then have the *ability* to do things that are sufficient for the occurrence in the past of things which did not in fact occur—for instance, to make a battle occur yesterday which did not occur. I still have the *ability*, in this sense, to read a certain kind of headline—my vision is all right, I know how to read, etc.—even though, due to the absence of some condition necessary for there being any such headline, I *cannot* do it.

Apply these considerations to Saunders's argument. The heart of his rejoinder is this:

> My knocking upon a thin wooden door with my fist is
> a sufficient condition for the door's shaking. Hence the

door's shaking is a necessary condition for my knocking upon the door. But the door's shaking is not a necessary condition for my *ability* to knock upon the door. (If it were, then my mere ability to knock upon the door would suffice to make it shake.) I may decide not to knock and the door may not shake, but it does not follow that I did not have it in my power to knock.

This is initially most persuasive, but to see how it fails, we need only to produce the same argument to show that I have it within my power to make something happen in the past which did not happen. Thus:

My reading a certain kind of headline is a sufficient condition for there being a naval battle yesterday. Hence there being a naval battle yesterday is a necessary condition for my reading such a headline. But the occurrence of such a battle is not a necessary condition for my *ability* to read such a headline. (If it were, then my mere ability to read such a headline would suffice to make the naval battle occur yesterday.) I may decide not to read such a headline and the battle may not have occurred yesterday, but it does not follow that I do not have it with my power to read such a headline.

Now if Saunders's argument against my fatalism is a good one, this argument refutes fatalism with respect to the past, for it is the *same* argument, with only a difference of tenses. But this argument obviously does not refute fatalism with respect to the past, nor does Saunders's argument refute it with respect to the future.

4

Fatalism and Linguistic Reform

JOHN TURK SAUNDERS

. . .I HAVE NO CHOICE..BUT to suppose that Taylor holds the following statement to be analytic [trivially true]: the only events which it is within one's power to produce are those which occur.

It is this which gives the fatalistic ring to his position. Caesar was stabbed and killed by Brutus and his colleagues, and a historian might think that it was in their power to bring about some situation alternative to Caesar's death, to have argued with him, compromised with him, etc. But on Taylor's view no such alternative was within their power. A frightening prospect indeed. Not only are we helpless creatures, but it is pointless to praise or blame us for not having brought about situations alternative to those which we do bring about: it is never in our power to do so. Though there is, perhaps, one redeeming feature to an otherwise sorry world: in order to enjoy whatever situations we might desire, we need not go to the trouble to bring them about; or, rather, to bring them about we have only to acquire the power to bring them about.

But before we begin to assess the advantages and disadvantages of the world which Taylor has unfolded before us, we had better stop to notice that he has told us nothing about the world at all. His position amounts to nothing more than the suggestion that we cease to use "in one's power" in the ordinary ways and begin to use it in his way. It is a suggestion for linguistic reform, but a "reform" which would bring upon us all of the inconveniences suggested by the preceding paragraph. In saying that it is within one's power to bring about a situation we ordinarily mean that he has the requisite skills and resources, that no one has bound him hand and foot to prevent his so doing, and so on. But Taylor has, in effect, recommended that we add a meaning rule to those which already govern "in one's power," *viz.*, the rule: if it is within one's power to bring about a situation then that situation occurs. And if we follow his recommendation we shall either become needlessly disturbed over the prospects mentioned in the preceding paragraph, or else we shall realize that Taylor has changed the meaning of "in one's power" and we shall revise its conceptually related terms ("helpless," "blameworthy," etc.) accordingly. (E.g., we shall cease to to use the terms "helpless" and "blameworthy" in such a way that if it was not in the power of Brutus and his friends to bring about some situation alternative to Caesar's death, they were helpless to do so, and deserve no blame for not doing so). We may follow Taylor's linguistic recommendation if we wish, though I see nothing but inconvenience as a consequence. The interesting, and perhaps frightening, fatalistic aura of Taylor's thesis lingers only so long as one fails to see that he has done nothing more awesome than to redefine an expression while continuing to employ it in its usual contexts. Small wonder that he arrives at strange results.

Lastly, I must address myself to Taylor's charge that, if my argument of the previous article refutes Taylor's fatalism, then it also refutes fatalism with respect to the past. . . . Let me, then, rephrase Taylor's charge. . . : if the non-occurrence of an event in the future does not entail my lack of power to bring about that event, then neither does the non-occurrence of an event in the past entail my lack of power to bring about the event. So phrased, I must say that I agree, at any rate to this extent: it is not due to the non-occurrence of an event in the past that I lack the power to bring about that event. I have no such power because we so use our language that it is false or nonsense to say that one has the power to bring about any event whatever in the past.

5

Fatalistic Arguments

WHILE JOHN TURK SAUNDERS expresses dismay at what he calls the "frightening prospect" of "the world which Taylor has unfolded before us," the crucial point is that Taylor's article is not an argument for fatalism. Rather, his essay claims that certain assumptions adopted almost universally in contemporary philosophy yield a proof of fatalism. Taylor leaves open the decision whether to accept fatalism or reject these assumptions. His preference, in fact, is to modify the law of excluded middle and view time as efficacious.

Saunders criticizes Taylor for equivocating in the use of the term "can," suggesting that Taylor confuses logical impossibility with "not having the power to." According to Saunders, the presupposition that no agent can perform any action in the absence of some condition necessary for its accomplishment expresses only an innocuous logical impossibility, and thus has nothing to do with what any agent is *able* to do. He argues that:

> My knocking upon a thin wooden door with my fist is a sufficient condition for the door's shaking. Hence the door's shaking is a necessary condition for my knocking upon the door. But the door's shaking is not a necessary condition for my *ability* to knock upon the door.

PART I: FATALISM

Taylor, however did not argue that no agent can *know how* to perform some act in the absence of some condition necessary for its accomplishment, and hence in *that* sense, does not have the ability to perform it. His point was, rather, that no matter what an agent might know how to do, he still cannot even do what he knows how to do (and is in that sense able to do) if lacking some condition necessary for doing it.

For example, imagine an expert pole-vaulter locked in a room with an eight-foot ceiling. Both Taylor and Saunders would agree that an expert pole-vaulter has the know-how or technical *expertise* to pole-vault twelve feet. In this sense of "can" the pole-vaulter can pole-vault twelve feet. What Taylor is asserting that, given the conditions of the locked room, it is not within the pole-vaulter's power to pole-vault twelve feet. The know-how is constrained by circumstances that prevent its being exercised.

Saunders dismisses as "strange" the view that "my mere ability to knock upon the door would suffice to make it shake." This view, however, is simply part of the fatalistic position. I cannot perform a given act if a necessary condition for doing so is lacking, no matter what I might know how to do, and this view does indeed imply, as Saunders points out, that if I can knock on the door then I shall. Strange as this claim may seem, fatalism is admittedly strange, and Taylor's argument for it can hardly be criticized for yielding a fatalistic conclusion.

Subsequently Saunders accuses Taylor of redefining "within one's power" while still employing the phrase in its usual contexts. Saunders claims that this "linguistic reform" accounts for Taylor's conclusion. According to Saunders, Taylor treats as analytic the view that "the only events which it is within one's power to produce are those which occur."

Taylor does not treat this statement as analytic. It does, however, follow from his argument and implies that the only actions one is able to perform are those one does perform—which is, again, fatalism.

Does this approach, though, amount to linguistic reform? I believe not. Consider a violinist who has forgotten to bring a violin to a recital and is unable at that time to obtain another. What Taylor is *not* asserting is that this violinist could not play the violin at the recital even if holding a violin. Such an assertion would be patently false. What Taylor *is* asserting is that if at the time of the recital the violinist does not have a violin, then at that time the violinist cannot present a recital with an imaginary violin. This statement, in contrast to the previous one, is obviously true, and in an ordinary sense of "cannot."

Taylor admits another sense of the word "can" which he does not utilize. Such is the notion of "know-how." In a sense of "can" the violinist without a violin can still play the violin, because the violinist knows how. Taylor does not use this sense of "can," however, because if this sense were to be utilized, fatalism with respect to the past would also be falsified.

Assume, for instance, that a sufficient condition for my having gone to a lecture yesterday is my having my own notes from it. Suppose that yesterday I did not go to the lecture. According to Taylor's use of "can," I cannot perform any act today sufficient for my having gone to the lecture yesterday, e.g., that it is not within my power today to read my notes from that lecture, because no such notes exist. No one disagrees, for we are all fatalists with respect to the past. We would not alter our belief if someone argued similarly to Saunders that actually I can perform an act sufficient for my having gone to the lecture yesterday, i.e., that I can read my notes from it, because I *know how* to read, open my notebook, and so on. No one accepts that meaning of "can" with respect to the past.

What Taylor has done is disregard that meaning of "can" with respect to the future also. He would claim that if I will not go to the lecture today, then I cannot perform any act sufficient for my attending it, and this claim is consistent with my knowing how to walk to the lecture hall, find a seat, and so on. Saunders's seemingly plausible claim that one can sometimes do something sufficient for the future occurrence of what is not going to happen is no more reasonable than the absurd claim that one can sometimes do something sufficient for the past occurrence of what did not happen.

Taylor has not engaged in linguistic reform. Rather he has utilized one sense of "can" which, in regard to the past, is consistent with everyone's use of the term. What he has tried to show is that this sense ought to be equally consistent with everyone's use of the word in regard to the future. Such is not the case, however, because people are unaware of their limitations with respect to the future but aware of them with respect to the past.

In a reply Taylor suggests that if Saunders's argument refutes fatalism in respect to the future, then it also refutes fatalism in respect to the past. Saunders denies this claim and asserts:

> . . .if the non-occurrence of an event in the future does not entail my lack of power to bring about that event, then neither does the non-occurrence of an event in the past entail my lack of power to bring about that event. . .[but] it is not due to the non-occurrence of an event in the past that I lack the power to bring about that event. I have no such power because we so use our language that it is false or nonsense to say that one has the power to bring about any event whatever in the past.

This reply, however, does not answer Taylor's charge. An expression possesses the meaning conferred by its use. The question why it is used as it is still remains. Has it an arbitrary use? Or does some actual difference between past and future account for the distinction? Saunders needs to point out such a difference, because Taylor's argument rests on denying it.

A common temptation is to respond to Taylor that while the past is closed and cannot be changed by our present actions, the future is open and can be affected by what we do. That observation, though, is not a refutation of Taylor's argument but accords with his view that while the claim that a naval battle will take place tomorrow is either true or false, it is not at present true and not at present false but only possible. Thus, as he puts it, time is "efficacious." Most philosophers reject this position, but Taylor's argument is designed to support it.

PART II

THEISM

Introduction

THE TERM "GOD" HAS been used in many ways, ranging from the Greek concept of the Olympian gods to the proposal by John Dewey that the divine is the "active relation between ideal and actual."[1] Let us adopt the more usual view that "God" refers to an all-good, all-powerful, all-knowing, creator of the world.

Much effort has been expended over the centuries seeking a proof for the existence of God, but even if no such effort succeeds, that result by itself fails to prove that God does not exist. To reach that conclusion requires a separate argument, and a much-debated one is the problem of evil.

Simply stated, the problem is that an all-good God would do everything possible to abolish evil. An all-powerful God would be able to abolish evil. Hence if an all-good, all-powerful God existed, evil would not. Yet evil exists. Therefore, an all-good, all-powerful God does not.

Can theists, those who believe in the existence of God, offer an explanation of why evil exists? One response, which some believe is suggested by the Book of Job, declares that the ways of God are mysterious and that words such as ""just" or "unjust" have no meaning when applied to God. Such is the approach suggested by Jack J. Cohen, a rabbi who served as director of the Hillel Foundation at the Hebrew University in Israel. This section begins with

1. John Dewey, *The Later Works of John Dewey, 1925–1953*, vol. 9, ed. Jo Ann Boydston (Carbondale: Southern Illinois University Press, 1988), 34.

his views, followed by my reply offering a different interpretation of the Book of Job that views it as doubting the goodness of God. Furthermore, I argue that if the meaning of the words we apply to God is unknown, then God is unknown.

Yet how important is belief in God? Louis P. Pojman, who was Professor of Philosophy at the United States Military Academy at West Point, maintains that theism gives special meaning to life, and I use his own words to outline his position. In response, I argue that even if God doesn't exist, our lives are not diminished. A world without God need not be a world without love.

Indeed, our situation would be unchanged even if the world had been created by an all-powerful, all-evil Demon, a view I call "the Moriarty hypothesis," named after the archenemy of Sherlock Holmes. I argue that whether you accept God or the Moriarty hypothesis, the more tenaciously you cling to your belief, the less important is its content. Indeed, if a hypothesis is interpreted to account for whatever events occur, then it becomes a dummy hypothesis, compatible with all possible facts and thus robbed of any explanatory power.

6

The Mystery of God

JACK J. COHEN

THE TOTAL MYSTERY OF God can be gleaned from the Book of Job. There we are presented with a deity whose workings in nature can in no way be inferred from a knowledge of nature's order. For how did that order come into existence? That is God's secret. Nor can man's moral intuitions be trusted. Job *knows* he is innocent, yet in the end he is satisfied to accept the dictate that the conventional-minded friends with whom he has carried on a courageous, honest debate are in a sense correct. Who is he, a mere mortal, to challenge God's justice? There is infinitely more to it than even his clear conscience can hope to fathom. Indeed he cannot any longer allow himself to think of God as just or unjust, at least as these terms are understood by man. These categories have no meaning when applied to God.

There is much in this conception of the author of Job and of other biblical passages to appeal to even the most stubborn unbeliever. In the first place, this conception takes account of the contradiction between fundamental beliefs of men abut right and wrong and the behavior of an all-powerful God who is at the same time all-good. It faces the problem squarely. And if the answer is given in the authoritative and overpowering rumble of a whirlwind rather than in the still small voice of reasoned analysis, there is at least no presumption that man's positive convictions about what is right are erroneous. The biblical conception of God limits the extent of man's ethical insights; it does not deny that within those limits he can suggest valid principles of conduct. Surely the most ardent modernist must reckon with man's inability to grasp completely the complexity of ethical behavior. We are still a long way from formulating a pattern of conduct which can harmonize all human values, however much we may be satisfied with the validity of many of them.

Secondly, the biblical view has the merit of admitting when it has reached the outer limits of understanding. God is described in anthropomorphic terms, but there is little question that at least the sophisticated portions of the Bible had abandoned anthropomorphic assumptions. The biblical God, in general, is a Power known only through His manifestations.

7

Job's Protest

JACK J. COHEN SUGGESTS that "The total mystery of God can be gleaned from the Book of Job." On the contrary, I would suggest that the Book reveals God's intentions, and they fail to justify God's actions. In any case, this memorable scriptural story merits careful attention.

Consider the plot. After a short introduction in which Job's exemplary piety and extraordinary good fortune are described, the scene shifts to heaven, where a dialogue takes place between God and Satan. God proudly comments to Satan about Job's great spiritual qualities. Satan scoffs at Job's devoutness, claiming that Job is obedient only because God has given Job good health, a fine family, and untold wealth. Although God testifies to Job's genuine piety, God permits Satan to test Job by inflicting on him the severest personal losses. Suddenly all ten of Job's children die, and his wealth is destroyed. When Job does not relinquish his faith in God, Satan, claiming that Job has maintained his faith only because his own body has been spared, obtains further permission from God to inflict on Job a most painful disease.

The scene now shifts to the land of Uz, the place of Job's residence. Having heard of his misfortunes, Job's three friends Eliphaz, Bildad, and Zophar come to comfort him. Job vents his feelings of despair, cursing the day he was born and avowing that under his circumstances death is better than life. Eliphaz advises Job to calm himself and not despise the chastening of the Almighty. Eliphaz believes that because Job is suffering, he must have sinned, for God does not punish the innocent. Eliphaz also counsels Job to repent for his sins and be restored to God's favor.

In response, Job points out that Eliphaz has not understood Job's outburst. Job has not lost faith in God. Rather, Job longs for death because his life has become intolerable. In a harsh rejoinder Bildad tells Job that God does not pervert justice, and that if Job were upright he would be prosperous. Job once again pleads with his friends that they do not understand the point of his complaint. He recognizes, as they do, the majesty of God, but Job claims to be innocent. He wishes only to know in what way he has erred, so that he might wholeheartedly repent. Finally Job cries out that he would willingly present his case before God, if the Almighty would only provide the opportunity.

The three friends and a newcomer, Elihu, repeat Eliphaz's basic argument: Job is suffering and therefore is a sinner, but if he would repent of his sins, God would pardon him. Job's response continues to be that although he claims innocence, he is prepared to be judged, and if found guilty, stands ready to accept just punishment.

The climax of the story comes when God answers Job from out of a whirlwind. God speaks of God's own wisdom and power in the creation and control of the mighty forces of nature. God points out the utter insignificance of humanity in the presence of God. God then questions Job's right even to inquire of God, for how could humanity ever hope to understand the workings of the Almighty? Finally, God urges Job to renew his faith in the wisdom, goodness, and justice of God, even though Job cannot hope to understand their workings.

In the divine presence Job is overawed. He humbles himself before God, promising never to inquire of God again but forever to believe fervently in the greatness and power of the Lord. The story concludes as God rebukes Eliphaz, Bildad, and Zophar for the advice they gave Job, pardoning them only out of regard for him. God heals Job, restores to him twice as much wealth as he had possessed before his misfortunes, and blesses him with ten children and a long and happy life.

Now let us examine the traditional interpretation of the Book of Job, which views it as a defense of God's power, knowledge, and goodness as well as an admission of human ignorance regarding the divine. Here is one such account:

> The Book of Job teaches us that God's ways are beyond the complete understanding of our little minds. Like Job, we must believe that God, who placed us in this world, knows what is best for us. Such faith in the goodness of God, even though we cannot altogether understand it, brings us strength and confidence to face our calamities and sorrows and sufferings.[1]

And here is another:

> The positive contribution of the Book of Job comes in the "Speeches of the Lord" which give Job something better than that which is provided by the feeble remarks of his friends. The essential point of these final speeches is that the problem is too great for the finite mind, that Job sees only a small segment of reality, and that his criticisms are accordingly inappropriate. How can Job know that either God's power or goodness is limited? His knowledge of temporal things is admittedly slight; his knowledge of eternal things is still more slight. The conclusion of the book is Job's recognition of his own humble status with the consequent mood of childlike trust.[2]

These variations on the basic interpretation, including that offered by Jack J. Cohen, overlook a key passage: the opening dialogue in heaven. If this scene were eliminated, the traditional understanding of the book would be persuasive. Readers would be in the place of Job. They would not know why he was suffering

1. Mortimer J. Cohen, *Pathways through the Bible* (Philadelphia: Jewish Publication Society of America, 1946), 460.

2. David Trueblood, *The Logic of Belief* (New York: Harper & Brothers, 1942), 293–294.

and would, like Job, be overawed by God's appearance from out of the whirlwind.

But readers are not in this position. We were told explicitly at the outset of the story why Job would suffer. Satan had, in effect, made a wager with God about the strength of Job's faith, and the wager required Job's suffering. God's words from out of the whirlwind at the climax of the plot appear childish when we are, in effect, behind the scenes. For God to have answered Job's question truthfully would have shown God to be anything but a great moral force. Does a righteous being make a wager involving human lives? Thus much in the manner of a bully who, when engaged in a philosophical dispute, challenges opponents to a fistfight to settle the issue, God attacks Job's position ad hominem, trying to disallow Job's right to ask an embarrassing question by emphasizing his inability to control nature.

Job does not possess God's power, but Job's question remains unanswered. Job may be overawed, but readers should not be, for we are aware of the circumstances surrounding God's actions. God's ways may be beyond Job's understanding, but they are not beyond the readers'. We can hardly be expected to have "childlike trust" in the goodness of a God who not only punishes Job unfairly but also without any possible justification kills his ten children. Had these individuals done anything unjust? Their lives were sacrificed as part of the wager. The ten children who are given to Job at the end of the story may to some extent compensate Job for his previous losses, but are the dead children compensated? Are they restored to life?

What, then, is the significance of the Book of Job? It stands opposed to the prevailing theology of almost all the rest of the Hebrew Bible. The doctrine of retributive justice, as presented in Deuteronomy, Psalms, Proverbs, and elsewhere, states that a pious person will be rewarded with wealth and happiness; a sinner will suffer both economic and physical adversity. Traditional believers supposed that the righteous were favored by God with material rewards, whereas sinners were punished with calamities. The Book of Job is a criticism of this theology. Later thinkers, however, could not accept this protest. They tried to twist the text into a pattern of orthodoxy. In effect, they turned a challenge to the righteousness of God's justice into a defense of unquestioning faith.

The Book of Job does not bolster the view that God's ways are mysterious; rather, it doubts that his actions are just. As such, the Book does not defend faith in the divine; to the contrary, it offers powerful support for skepticism about such faith.

8

The Problem of Meaning

Is GOD, IN JACK J. Cohen's words, a "total mystery?" Do the categories of just or unjust "have no meaning when applied to God"? To adopt this position is fatal to theism, for how can we make sense of the view that something exists if it is a total mystery?

Suppose, for instance, we are asked whether we believe in the existence of a "snark."[1] We inquire what a snark is, what specific characteristics it possesses. If we are told its nature is unknowable, what would be the sense of our affirming or denying its existence? About what would be talking? Belief in the existence of a wholly incomprehensible snark is empty. So is belief in the existence of a wholly incomprehensible God.

To avoid this pitfall, theists may claim that we do have some knowledge of God's nature, because, for example, we know God is wise and just, although the words "wise" and "just" have a different meaning when applied to God than when applied to human beings. What is this meaning? One possible answer is that no one knows. This reply, however, leads to a dead end, for we cannot speak intelligently using words we don't understand. If the

1. I take the term from Lewis Carroll's humorous poem "The Hunting of the Snark: An Agony, in Eight Fits," reprinted in *Alice in Wonderland*, ed. Donald J. Gray (New York: Norton, 1971), 213–30.

meaning of the words we apply to God is unknown, then God is unknown.

One traditional response to this difficulty is to maintain that God's attributes cannot be conceived in positive terms but only negatively. For example, to say that "God knows" is to deny that God does not know. This approach is supposed to make possible the avoidance of applying human concepts to the divine essence.

But to deny that someone does not possess knowledge is to affirm that the individual possesses knowledge. If that implication fails to hold, than we do not understand the meaning of our own words. and we cannot use them to make meaningful claims.

If God's knowledge has nothing in common with human knowledge, then, as the heterodox medieval Jewish philosopher Gersonides (Levi ben Gershom) argued, we might as well say that God lacks knowledge, adding the proviso that the term "knowledge" applied to God does not have the same meaning as it does ordinarily.[2] In other words, once we allow ourselves to use words without being able to offer any explanation of them, we might as well say anything, for none of what we say makes any sense.

What if the words we apply to God are to be taken not literally but metaphorically? Does that approach help deal with the problem? Only if the metaphors can be explained in non-metaphorical language. Otherwise, we are attempting to elucidate a mystery by means of an enigma.

To see how a normal metaphor can be unpacked, consider an example offered by Janet Martin Soskice, who has developed a sophisticated defense of the use of metaphor in speaking of God. Commenting on e. e. cumming's line "nobody, not even the rain, has such small hands," she proposes that "the power of the metaphor rests in its casting up in the reader's mind thoughts of what kinds of hands rain might have, suggestions of fragility, delicacy, transience, ability to reach the smallest places." Thus does Soskice intend to show that a metaphor may offer "a new vision, the birth of a new understanding, a new referential access."

2. Levi ben Gershom, *The Wars of the Lord*, trans. Seymour Feldman (Philadelphia: Jewish Publication Society, 1987), 2:111.

She stresses that science as well as literature uses metaphor. In both cases, the figure of speech arises from a model, which she defines as "an object or state of affairs viewed in terms of its resemblance, real or hypothetical, to some other object or state of affairs." The brain may thus be modeled on a computer, leading to talk of "programming," "inputs" and "feedback."

If, however, theological models are analogous to scientific ones, shouldn't the former, like the latter, be causally explanatory, falsifiable, and revisable? Soskice agrees, arguing that "the Christian realist must concede that there is a point, theoretically at least, at which he would be committed to surrendering his theism."[3] But where is this point? The question is invariably left unanswered.

In offering her account of e. e. cumming's line, Soskice explains its metaphor in non-metaphorical language. After she does, the metaphor yields the non-metaphorical assertion that the rain is delicate and transient. If that rain is part of a hurricane, then the claim is false.

Can theological metaphors also be explained so as to yield non-metaphorical claims? If so, we can speak of God literally, a position theists typically seek to deny.

If the metaphors cannot be explained, however, why is one more appropriate than another? We talk of God the Father or possibly God the Mother. But why not God the Aunt or Uncle, God the Cousin, or God the Neighbor? Some may protest that these phrases are inexplicable. Perhaps so. But one inexplicable metaphor is as good as another.

Thus we are left with the problem of meaning. How can we sensibly affirm the existence of an incomprehensible God?

3. Janet Martin Soskice, *Metaphor and Religious Language* (Oxford: Clarendon Press, 1985), 57–58, 101, 140.

9

Theism and Meaning

LOUIS P. POJMAN

IF THEISM IS TRUE and there is a benevolent supreme being governing the universe, the following eight theses are true.

1. We have a satisfying explanation of the origin and sustenance of the universe. We are not the product of chance and necessity or an impersonal big bang, but of a Heavenly Being who cares about us.

2. [T[he universe is suffused in goodness and. . .good will win out over evil. We are not fighting a desperate battle alone, but God is on our side—or rather, it is possible to be on God's side in the struggle of good over evil.

3. God loves and cares for us. His love compels us, so that we have a deeper motive for morally good action.

4. [T]he love of God. . . guarantees justice, so that you will get what you deserve—good for good and bad for bad.

5. Cosmic justice reigns in the universe. . ..[E]ach will be judged according to how one has used one's talents.

6. All persons are of equal worth. Since we have all been created in the image of God and are His children, we are all brothers and sisters.

7. The moral guilt which we experience, even for the most heinous acts, can be removed, and we can be redeemed and given a new start.

8. There is life after death. Death is not the end of the matter, but we shall live on, recognizing each other in a better world.[1]

Of course, the problem is that we probably do not know if theism, let alone our particular religious version of it, is true. . .[I]t is in our interest to live as though it were true, to consider each person as a child of God, of high value, to work as though God is working with us in the battle of good over evil, and to build a society based on these ideas.

---

1. For my views on the concept of heaven, see "Heaven" in *The Road Traveled and Other* Essays, the first volume of this trilogy.

10

Life Without God

LOUIS P. POJMAN SUGGESTS that if we do not believe in God, our lives are diminished. Why accept this view? After all, even if God does not exist, we are still alive, as are others we cherish, we still experience times of health and sickness, we still strive to achieve goals, we still relish successes and regret failures, we still witness inspiring acts of goodness and disheartening deeds of evil, and we still face moral problems and have to make difficult decisions.

Granted, we cannot expect help from God. Even if God exists, however, our choices are our own, not God's. We cannot look to God for guidance, because what God wills is unknown. We cannot rest secure in the belief that God is taking care of us, for the existence of God is consistent with the occurrence of all manner of tragedy.

Would life without God lack meaning? The answer depends on what sort of meaning a life can have. If a meaningful life is taken to be one in which each individual plays a role in a divine drama, entering and exiting the stage at an appointed time in order to serve God's purposes, then in the absence of God, life has no meaning.

Why assume, however, that people cannot have their own purposes, independent of any divine playwright? Suppose I wish to devote my life to teaching philosophy, you wish to devote your life to providing medical care to the sick, and others wish to devote their lives to composing music, cultivating a garden, or raising a family. Why aren't these activities meaningful? None of them depends on the existence of God. They nevertheless provide life with significance. They are freely chosen, not preordained, but so much the better. They are expressions of our own personalities and values.

Or is the problem supposed to be that in the absence of God we are unable to decide which values or moral principles to accept? This challenge can be met by using reason to assess specific ethical judgments in the light of shared human concerns and our common experience.

To illustrate the process, let us consider in turn various moral principles that have been thought by many to embody the will of God but that, regardless of whether God exists, fall short of providing an entirely satisfactory foundation for morality. These rules, whatever their origin, are not immune from difficulties that can be recognized by theists and nontheists alike.

Consider the Golden Rule, a principle endorsed by various religious traditions. Its positive formulation, attributed to Jesus, is: "In everything do to others as you would have them do to you."[1] The negative formulation, which appeared at least five centuries earlier, is attributed to Confucius and was later proposed by the Jewish sage Hillel. The latter put it as follows: "What is hateful to you, do not to your neighbor."[2] Is either of these versions entirely acceptable?

Consider first the positive formulation. Granted, we usually should treat others as we would wish them to treat us. For instance, we should go to the aid of an injured person, just as we would wish that person to come to our aid if we were injured. If we always followed this rule, however, the results would be unfortunate.

1. Matthew 7:12 The translation, as all subsequent ones from the New Testament, is from *The Holy Bible: New Revised Standard Version* (New York: Oxford University Press, 1989).

2. *Babylonian Talmud* (London: Soncino Press, 1938), Shabbath, 31a.

Masochists, for instance, derive pleasure from being hurt. Were they to act according to the principle in question, their duty wold be to inflict pain, thereby doing to others as they wish done to themselves. Similarly, consider a person who enjoys receiving telephone calls, regardless of who is calling. The principle would require that person to telephone everyone, thereby reciprocating preferred treatment. Indeed, strictly speaking, to fulfill the positive formulation of the Golden Rule would be impossible, because we wish so many to do so much for us that we would not have time to do all that is necessary to treat them likewise. As the philosopher Walter Kaufman commented, "anyone who tried to live up to Jesus' rule would become an insufferable nuisance."[3]

In this respect, the negative formulation of the Golden Rule is preferable, because it does not imply that we have innumerable duties toward everyone else. Neither does it imply that masochists ought to inflict pain on others, nor that those who enjoy receiving telephone calls ought themselves to make calls. While the negative formulation does not require these actions, however, neither does it forbid them. It enjoins us not to do to others what is hateful to ourselves, but pain is not hateful to the masochist and innumerable calls are not hateful to the telephone enthusiast. Thus the negative formulation, though superior in one way to the positive formulation, is not without weakness, because it does not prohibit actions that ought to be prohibited.

Whether the Golden Rule in either formulation is supposed to be of divine origin makes no difference in our assessment. All can agree that, whatever its source, the principle does not by itself serve as the ultimate moral touchstone.

Even the Ten Commandments, accepted by adherence of a variety of religions, also have their limitations. Consider the Second Commandment, which, after prohibiting the making or serving of sculptured images, goes on to say: "For I the LORD your God am an impassioned God, visiting the guilt of the parents upon the children, upon the third and upon the fourth generations

3. Walter Kaufman, *The Faith of a Heretic* (New York: Doubleday, 1963), 212.

of those who reject Me, but showing kindness to the thousandth generation of those who love Me and keep My commandments."[4] But to punish one person for the moral lapses of another is unethical, as is rewarding a person for the good deeds of another. This point was made emphatically by the prophet Ezekiel, who declared: "A child shall not share the burden of a parent's guilt, nor shall a parent share the burden of a child's guilt; the righteousness of the righteous shall be accounted to him alone."[5] Incidentally, Ezekiel's principle rules out the possibility that anyone, including God, could act in such a way as to absolve us of our responsibility for our failings. If we act immorally, we are to blame.

The Fifth Commandment instructs individuals to honor their father and mother. Suppose, however, parents break the Second Commandment by making and worshipping sculptured images. Or perhaps they break some of the remaining commandments by coveting a neighbor's property, bearing false witness, stealing, engaging in adultery, or even committing murder. Although they might still merit their child's concern, parents who acted in such ways would not deserve to be honored.

Two of the commandments take slavery for granted. The Fourth, which requires individuals to remember the Sabbath day and keep it holy, prohibits work at that time by "you, your son or daughter, your male or female slave."[6] The Tenth prohibits coveting anything that belongs to a neighbor, including his "wife, or his male or female slave."[7] Slavery we all now agree is unethical, yet the Ten Commandments treats it as an acceptable practice.

A further problem is that the Commandments are stated as if they allowed no exceptions. Yet under certain circumstances, not to break a Commandment would be widely regarded as immoral. For example, if a young girl's life depended on her mother's stealing

4. Exodus 20:5–6. The translation, as all subsequent ones from the Hebrew Bible, is from *Tanakh: The Holy Scriptures* (Philadelphia: Jewish Publication Society, 1985.)

5. Ezekial 18: 20.

6. Exodus 21:10.

7. Exodus 20:14.

a small amount of money from a wealthy, immoral person, most would view the theft favorably.

Not only do certain circumstances call for making exceptions to the Commandments, but situations can develop in which fulfilling one Commandment would amount to breaking another. If, for instance, a man had to work on the Sabbath in order to take his critically ill father to the hospital, the Commandment to honor one's father and mother would take precedence over the Commandment not to work on the Sabbath. The Commandments have exceptions but do not themselves provide any guidance for when or how to make such exceptions. Thus regardless of claims of their divine origin and despite their moral worth, the Ten Commandments fall short as an ultimate guide to morality.

The same is true of the sacred Christian text, the Sermon on the Mount. Amid its beauties of language and thought, we find such an unacceptable principles as "[I]f your right hand cause you to sin, cut it off and throw it away. . ."[8] Any statement, of course, can be interpreted to render it sensible, but taken literally, thieves cutting off their hands would be acts of lunacy. If the statement is not to be taken literally, however, it does not provide an unambiguous guide to moral action.

A similar problem is implicit in Jesus's instruction that "whoever marries a divorced woman commits adultery."[9] Few would find such a principle morally acceptable. What of Jesus's saying, "[D]o not worry about your life, what you will eat or what you will drink. . ."[10] Wouldn't such a lack of concern for oneself be a sign of a psychological problem as well as an unfair drain on family and friends?

If these sayings appear peripheral to Jesus's principal message, consider this central passage: "Do not resist an evildoer. But if anyone strikes you on the right cheek, turn the other also; and if anyone wants to sue you and take your coat, give your cloak as

8. Matthew 5:30.
9. Matthew 5:32.
10. Matthew 6:25.

well. . ."[11] The difficulty is that, in order to avoid the triumph of evil, those who adhere to such pacifism depend on others not adhering to it. Turning the other cheek to a Stalin is death. Not to fight for the right is wrong. Throughout history, when those who consider themselves devout Christians have come under attack, they have temporarily put aside the Sermon on the Mount and picked up their weapons. To have done otherwise would have led to the destruction of Christianity. Recall that when Jesus entered Jerusalem, he "drove out all who were selling and buying in the temple, and he overturned the tables of the money changers and the seats of those who sold doves."[12] So much for turning the other cheek.

Over the course of centuries many persons have found the Golden Rule, the Ten Commandments, or the Sermon on the Mount inspirational and worthy of devotion. Yet these statements of principle, like all others, require interpretation by the use of reason, and testing by appeal to the lessons of experience. If God exists, our principles, even if attributed to the divine, still need to be evaluated. Theism doesn't solve our moral problems. And even if God does not exist, we may still commit ourselves to care for others. A world without God need not be a world without love.

11. Matthew 5:39.
12. Matthew 21:12.

11

The Moriarty Hypothesis

LOUIS P. POJMAN DESCRIBES the world as viewed by a theist, that is, one who believes in an omnipotent, all-good God. Yet how different would be the perspective of a demonist, that is, one who believes in an omnipotent, all-evil Demon? Surprisingly, both have the same expectations about the events of this world. In other words, both demonists and theists may choose to interpret their contrary views as supported equally by any future occurrences, no matter how good or evil they may be.

To illustrate this admittedly counterintuitive claim, consider the fictional examples of Sherlock Holmes and his archenemy, Professor Moriarty. Holmes believed that Moriarty was the "great malignant brain" behind crime in London, the "deep organizing power" that unified "every deviltry" into "one connected whole," the "foul spider which lurks in the center," "never caught—never so much as suspected."[1] Now suppose Moriarty's power extended throughout the universe, so that all events (perhaps excluding acts of human freedom) were the work of one all-powerful, all-evil Demon. Let us call this theory the "Moriarty hypothesis."

1. Arthur Conan Doyle, *The Complete Sherlock Holmes* (Garden City, NY: Doubleday, n.d.), 471, 496, 769. The works cited are "The Final Problem," "The Adventure of the Norwood Builder, and "The Valley of Fear."

Does the presence of various goods refute the Moriarty hypothesis? No, for just as theism can be presumed to be consistent with the world's most horrendous evils, so the Moriarty hypothesis can be presumed to be consistent with the world's most wondrous goods. While any evil can be viewed as logically necessary for a greater good, any good can be viewed as logically necessary for a greater evil. Thus the Moriarty hypothesis is not obviously false.

Now consider the following two assessments of the human condition:

1. "Is not all life pathetic and futile?. . .We reach. We grasp. And what is left in our hands at the end? A shadow. Or worse than a shadow—misery."

2. "The first entrance into life gives anguish to the newborn infant, and to its wretched parent; weakness, impotence, distress attend each stage of that life, and it is, at last, finished in agony and horror."

Which is the viewpoint of a theist and which that of a believer in the Moriarty hypothesis? As it happens, (1) is uttered by Sherlock Holmes,[2] and (2) by the orthodox believer Demea in Hume's *Dialogues concerning Natural Religion*.[3] The positions appear interchangeable.

Both the theist and the believer in the Moriarty hypothesis recognize that life contains happiness as well as misery. No matter how terrible the misery, the theists may regard it as unsurprising; after all, aren't all evils, in principle, explicable? To believers in the Moriarty hypothesis, happiness may be regarded as unsurprising; after all, aren't all goods, in principle, explicable? Supporters of both positions are apt to view events that appear to conflict with their fundamental principles merely as test of fortitude, opportunities to display strength of commitment.

If defenders of either view modified their beliefs in the light of changing circumstances, then their expectations would differ.

2. Doyle, "The Adventure of the Retired Colourman," 1113.

3. David Hume, *Dialogues concerning Natural Religion*, ed. Dorothy Coleman (New York: Cambridge University Press, 2007), 10:8.

But believers are loath to admit doubt. They admire those who stand fast in their faith, regardless of appearances.

Any seemingly contrary evidence can be considered ambiguous. St. Paul says, "we see in a mirror, dimly,"[4] and Sherlock Holmes speaks of seeking the truth "through the veil which shrouded it."[5] If events are so difficult to interpret, they provide little reason for believers to abandon deep-seated tenets. Those who vacillate are typically viewed by other members of their communities as weakhearted and faithless.

One other attempt to differentiate the expectations of the theist and the believer in the Moriarty hypothesis is to suppose that theists have reason to be more optimistic than their counterparts. This presumption, however, is unwarranted. Recall these words from the Book of Ecclesiastes: "Then I accounted those who died long since more fortunate than those who are still living; and happier than either are those who have not yet come into being and have never witnessed the miseries that go on under the sun."[6] A more pessimistic view is hard to imagine.

We may be living, as the theist supposes, in the best of all possible worlds, but if so, the best of all possible worlds contains immense torments. On the other hand, we may be living, as the believer in the Moriarty hypothesis supposes, in the worst of all possible worlds, but if so, the worst of all possible worlds contains enormous delights. Both scenarios offer us reason to be cheerful and reason to be gloomy. Our outlook depends on our personalities, not our theology or demonology.

Thus as we seek to understand life's vicissitudes, does our view depend on whether we believe in God or in the Moriarty hypothesis? Not if we hold either of these beliefs unshakably. For the more tenaciously we cling to our belief, the less important is its content.

4. I Corinthians 13:12.

5. Doyle, "The Final Problem," 471.

6. Ecclesiastes 4:2–3..

12

Dummy Hypotheses

To HOLD TO AN explanation of events in the face of conflicting facts is not to protect one's view but to render it pointless. As an illustration of this principle, consider the following anecdote found in Anita Shreve's novel *All He Ever Wanted:*

> A man is propelled one minute sooner to his automobile because he decides not to stop to kiss his wife good-bye. As a consequence of this omission, he then crosses a bridge one minute before it collapses, taking all its traffic and doomed souls into the swilling and angry depths below. Oblivious, and safely out of harm's way, our man continues on his journey.[1]

Let us first suppose this man is a theist and, when he becomes aware of his good fortune attributes it to the benevolence of God, or, as Louis P. Pojman puts it, 'Cosmic justice.' What are we to make of the claim?

To begin with, whatever goodness God displayed in this man's case did not extend to the many others who fell to their death. How is God's benevolence compatible with such a tragedy?

1. Anita Shrive, *All He Ever Wanted* (Boston: Little, Brown, and Company, 2003), 79.

Our man does not know, but when he ponders the matter, he is likely to suppose that the chain of events serves a divine purpose that lies beyond human understanding.

Suppose next that this man does not believe in the existence of God but, instead, accepts the Moriarty hypothesis, thus attributing events to the malevolence of the Demon. What are we to make of this claim?

To begin with, whatever evil the Demon displayed in these horrific events did not extend to the man himself, for he was saved. How is the Demon's malevolence compatible with this man's good fortune? He does not know, but when he ponders the matter, he is likely to suppose that the chain of events serves a demonic purpose that lies beyond human understanding.

A third hypothesis the man might accept is that the world is the scene of a struggle between God and the Demon (or as Zoroastrians view it, a cosmic war between Ahura Mazda, the source of all good, and Ahriman, the source of all evil.) Assume both God and the Demon are powerful, but neither is omnipotent. When events go well, God's benevolence is in the ascendancy; when events go badly, the Demon's malevolence is in the ascendancy. In the tragic case under consideration the Demon caused the collapse of the bridge while God arranged for the one man to be saved.

Is this third explanation unnecessarily complex and therefore to be rejected? No, for even though in one sense it is more complex than the other two, because it involves two supernatural beings rather than only one, in another sense the third explanation is simpler than the other two, because it leaves no aspect of the situation beyond human understanding.

The crucial point is that all three hypotheses (as well as innumerable others one might imagine) can be maintained regardless of the facts. For instance, suppose the bridge had collapsed at a time when all vehicles but one had already crossed. Then the theist would thank God for having saved the lives of so many, while considering mysterious why the one vehicle was lost; the believer in the Moriarty hypothesis would attribute the loss of the one vehicle to the work of the Demon, while considering mysterious why the lives of so many were saved; the believer in God and the Demon would thank God for having saved the lives of so many, while attributing the loss of the one vehicle to the work of the Demon.

Any of these incompatible hypotheses can be interpreted to account for whatever events occur. Using them in this way turns them into dummy hypotheses, compatible with all possible facts. Like a dummy bell rope that makes no sound, a dummy hypothesis makes no sense. Its compatibility with all possible situations robs it of any explanatory power.

Contrast a dummy hypothesis with a scientific one, which is typically tested by the following four-step procedure: (1) Formulate the hypothesis clearly; (2) Work out the implications of the hypothesis; (3) Perform controlled experiments to verify whether these implications hold; (4) Observe the consequences of these experiments and, as a result, accept or reject the hypothesis. In practice, complications may abound at each stage, and any of the assumptions made for the purpose of the experiment may be challenged. Furthermore, the method yields only high probabilities, not certainties, for a hypothesis may pass numerous tests yet fail additional ones. The crucial point, however, is that scientific hypotheses are tested, then rejected if inconsistent with the outcome of the tests.

As an example of how scientific method works, consider the case of the American army surgeon Dr. Walter Reed, who sought to control yellow fever. He hypothesized that the disease was caused by a specific type of mosquito. To test this hypothesis, he quarantined some individuals so that they would not come into contact with any of the insects, but did not quarantine the other test subjects. When those exposed developed the disease and those quarantined did not, Reed had strong evidence that the mosquitoes were the cause of the disease.

Had the results of the experiment been different, Reed's hypothesis might have turned out to be false. If those quarantined had developed the disease at the same rate as those exposed, then Reed would have rejected his hypothesis and been led to develop and test others.

That a hypothesis can be disproved by testing is not a weakness of the hypothesis but a strength. Any genuine hypothesis is open to possible refutation. Dummy hypotheses are not and thus do not provide understanding. They may be psychologically comforting but do not enable us to gain control over our environment.

Some may choose to attribute an outbreak of yellow fever to God (or cosmic justice), the Demon (or cosmic injustice), or a conflict between them. Such hypotheses are untestable, however, and therefore do not help eradicate or control the disease.

Finally, a few thoughts abut the story of the fallen bridge with which we began. Why did it collapse? The answer is most likely to be found by calling in engineers who can determine the cause, learn from the case, and build a new bridge that will be safer. At no point, however, will they rely on theories involving cosmic clashes or divine and demonic beings.

Yet some may persist in asking why the one man was saved. The answer is that he arrived one minute sooner because of not stopping to kiss his wife good-bye. Why didn't he kiss his wife good-bye? Perhaps he was distracted by thoughts of an upcoming business meeting. Why was that meeting so critical? We can continue such speculation endlessly, but the key point is that no question we may raise will be answered satisfactorily by appealing to any dummy hypothesis.

PART III

HAPPINESS

Introduction

CAN AN IMMORAL PERSON be happy? The answer to this question divides philosophers. Some believe that only those who act morally can find satisfaction in life; others find this claim unrealistic.

The background to this long-standing debate is provided in the selection by Robert B. Talisse, Professor of Philosophy at Vanderbilt University. He explains how the matter goes back to the writings of Aristotle, who maintained that happiness can only be attained by those who act in accordance with moral virtue.

But what about the case of someone who is apparently happy but acts immorally? In "The Happy Immoralist" I describe such a person whom I name "Fred," an acronym derived from the words "fame," "riches," "esteem," and "deceit." Critics, however, argue that while Fred "feels happy," he is not "truly happy" and has not attained "real happiness."

This view is defended by John Kleinig, Professor Emeritus of Philosophy at John Jay College of Criminal Justice and the Graduate Center of the City University of New York. He argues that Fred's happiness is "chimerical." As Kleinig puts it, "We know what a wretch [Fred] is, and Fred would be troubled, too, if he knew that we knew."

The late Jeffrey G. Murphy was Professor of Law, Philosophy, and Religious Studies in the Sandra Day O'Connor College of Law at Arizona State University. He claimed that Fred "may indeed be happy in some limited way" but not "in the full sense." Indeed,

Murphy expressed pity for Fred, because "he is punished by being the kind of person that he is."

Christopher W. Gowans, Professor of Philosophy at Fordham University, doubts that Fred is happy. Perhaps superficially he is, but he lacks "real happiness." Were he an actual person, we would have reason to suspect that he is "anxious and lonely."

Christine Vitrano, professor of philosophy at Brooklyn College of the City University of New York with whom I authored a book on living well,[1] takes issue with those who believe Fred could not be happy. After commenting on the views of Kleinig, Murphy, and Gowans, she maintains that philosophers who deny Fred's happiness are using the word "happy" in an unusual way. Indeed, she argues: "Being happy implies nothing about the value of a person's life independent of her own perceptions."

In support of Vitrano's position, I present two cases of happy immoralists. The first is based on the protagonist in Woody Allen's movie *Crimes and Misdemeanors*, who agrees to a murder in order to save his marriage, professional life, and reputation.

Granted that case is fictional, but the final one I offer is not. It is that of Richard Rich, a figure in English history, dramatized in the play and movie *A Man for All Seasons*, who committed perjury in court, performed many other immoral acts, and became Speaker of the House of Commons and Lord Chancellor of England. He was highly unethical, yet he fulfilled his ambitious goals, and the evidence suggests he was a happy person.

1. Steven M. Cahn and Christine Vitrano, *Happiness and Goodness: Philosophical Reflections on Living Well* (New York: Columbia University Press, 2015).

13

Understanding the Debate

ROBERT B. TALISSE

PROFESSOR: Why have you enrolled in my course?
STUDENT: Because it's required for my major.
PROFESSOR: But why are you doing what's required for your major?
STUDENT: Because I want to complete my degree.
PROFESSOR: But why do you want to complete your degree?
STUDENT: Because I want to get a good job.
PROFESSOR: But why do you want to get a good job?
STUDENT: Because I want to earn a good salary.
PROFESSOR: But why do you want to earn a good salary?
STUDENT: So that I can afford to buy the things I want— nice house, a fast car, delicious food, fashionable clothes, and so on.
PROFESSOR: But why do you want those things?
STUDENT: Because having them will make me happy.
PROFESSOR: But why do you want to be happy?
student: Huh?

PART III: HAPPINESS

IT WAS PROBABLY ARISTOTLE who first took note of the special role that the concept of happiness plays in our thinking about how to live. Happiness, he argued, is the final end of all human activity, that for the sake of which every action is performed. The Student is perplexed at the end of the exchange above because the Professor, in posing her final question, betrays a lack of familiarity with this basic Aristotelian insight. The Student understands that there really is no response to the question "Why do you want to be happy?" To identify an action as necessary for one's happiness is to explain why one would even perform it. When explaining human action, happiness is where the buck stops.

Aristotle's insight seems undeniable and, understandably, it remains popular among philosophers. However, like most undeniable philosophical claims, it ultimately does not tell us much. To identify happiness as the definitive aim of human action is to simply assert that we do what we think will bring us happiness. It is to say that when we act, we act for the sake of *what we take to be* happiness. As appearances can be deceiving, deep questions persist about what happiness is.

Perhaps this is why Aristotle affirmed further that happiness is the culmination of all of the good things a human life could manifest. He claimed that the truly happy person not only derives great enjoyment from living, but is also both morally and cognitively flawless. In fact, Aristotle goes so far as to posit that the happy person necessarily has friends, good looks, health, and wealth. And, as if these advantages were not enough, he holds that the fully happy person is invulnerable even to misfortune and bad luck. According to Aristotle, then, happiness is not simply that for the sake of which we act; it is that which renders a human life complete, lacking nothing that could improve it.

Few philosophers today subscribe to Aristotle's view that complete success in every evaluative dimension is strictly required for happiness. Most will readily concede that a person could be happy and yet not especially intelligent, beautiful, or wealthy; some even argue that a happy life typically involves various kinds of deficiency. Still, a slightly more modest version of Aristotle's second claim continues to be influential among contemporary moral philosophers. This is the idea that the immoral person is necessarily unhappy, that morality is necessary for happiness.

The attraction of this view is easy to discern. Since Plato, moral philosophers have been embroiled in a confrontation with immoralism, which is the view that morality is some kind of sham. The immoralist's challenge is often posed as a simple question: "Why be moral?" In asking this, the immoralist demands an account of why one should be *motivated* to act according to morality's demands, especially given that to do so is often burdensome. Interestingly, most versions of immoralism accept Aristotle's initial claim that happiness is the ultimate aim of human action, and they typically accept the further thought that happiness renders one's life successful as well. What the immoralist denies, then, is that anyone has a good reason to be moral. However, if it could be shown that being moral is necessary for happiness, then immoralism would be defeated. The moralist's argument against immoralism looks simple enough: One aims ultimately to be happy, and morality is necessary for happiness; therefore, one has sufficient reason to be moral. Again, the buck stops with happiness.

Contemporary moral philosophers tend to presuppose the success of some version of this simple argument. Others, however, oppose this line of reasoning. Their central thesis can be put succinctly: Morality is not necessary for happiness. The immoral person might be a completely happy person, and the moral saint might nonetheless be absolutely miserable.

Thus the issue is joined. By exploring it we learn something about happiness and morality but most of all about ourselves.

14

The Happy Immoralist

ACCORDING TO THE BRITISH philosopher Philippa Foot, "happiness is a most intractable concept." She commits, herself, however to the claim that "great happiness, unlike euphoria or even great pleasure, must come from something related to what is deep in human nature, and fundamental in human life, such as affection for children and friends, the desire to work, and love of freedom and truth."[1] I am not persuaded by this characterization of happiness and offer the following counterexample.

Consider Fred, a fictitious person but an amalgamation of several individuals I have known. Fred's life has been devoted to achieving three aims: fame, wealth, and a reputation for probity. He has no interest whatsoever in friends or truth. Indeed, he is treacherous and thoroughly dishonest. Nevertheless, he has attained his three goals and is, in fact, a rich celebrity renowned for his supposed integrity. His acquiring a good name while acting unscrupulously is a tribute to his audacity, cunning, and luck. Now he rests self-satisfied: basking in renown, delighting in luxuries,

---

1. Philippa Foot, "Moral Relativism," in *Moral Dilemmas and Other Topics in Moral Philosophy* (Oxford: Clarendon, 2002), 35.

and relishing praise for his reputed commitment to the highest moral standards.

That he enjoys great pleasure, even euphoria, is undeniable. According to Philippa Foot, however, he is not happy. I would say, rather, that *we* are not happy with *him*. We do not wish to see shallowness and hypocrisy rewarded. Indeed, while numerous works of literature describe good persons who are doomed to failure, few works tell of evil persons who ultimately flourish. (An exception to the rule is Natasha in Chekhov's *The Three Sisters*, a play that causes most audiences anguish.)

We can define "happiness" so as to falsify the claim that Fred is happy. This philosophical sleight-of-hand, though, accomplishes little, for Fred is wholly contented, suffering no worries or anxieties. Indeed, he is smug, as he revels in his exalted position.

Happiness may be, as Philippa Foot says, an "intractable concept," Yet surely Fred is happy. Perhaps later in life he won't be. Or perhaps he will. He may come to the end of his days as happy as he is now. I presume his case provides a reason why God is supposed to have created hell, for if Fred suffers no punishment in the next world, he may escape punishment altogether. And believing in that prospect is yet another reason he is happy.

15

Happiness and Virtue

JOHN KLEINIG

WE MIGHT WONDER WHY Steven Cahn's character Fred in his essay "The Happy Immoralist" is fictitious—why he had to be an amalgam. Is it that, given the world are we know it, a real Fred would almost certainly have had an exceedingly short half-life? One must presume, for example, that, even if Fred dies happily in his sleep, his desire for fame and reputation did not include a historical legacy. If it did, Cahn has now unmasked him, and we see that Fred's happiness was epistemically unsound. Had he realized. . .

To be sure, happiness is agent-relative, but happiness as a judgment on the satisfactoriness of one's life—-that it is well with one—is more than a state of euphoria and even of ongoing pleasure. It is a recognition that the various parts of one's life are functioning well in a coherent and stable fashion, that one's important goals are being accomplished, and that one is satisfied with how they are being accomplished. It may well be that Fred possesses sufficient cunning to ensure that—at least during his lifetime—his fame, wealth, and reputation remain intact in spite of the way they have been achieved, and that he does not particularly care about what will be learned about him after his death. It may also be the case—though this is a bit of a psychological stretch—that Fred is beset by no anxieties about the fragility of his psychosocial world. One would ordinarily think that someone with Fred's cunning might well be troubled by the possibility of other Freds or even re-silient and persistent victims of his treachery. Machiavelli's Prince is more believable than Cahn's Fred.

But let us take Fred as we have been given him. What do we say? I guess we can say, "Yes, one or two Freds may make it. But if happiness is to be seen as a *human* goal, Fred's path to success is an extremely perilous one. And if that's all you want—to make it like Fred, die happy in your sleep, and have a devil-may-care attitude about what people think *after* you're gone, well and good."

For most of us—and it has to be for most of us—happiness is bound up with living a life very different from Fred's. We may cavil at the details of Philippa Foot's account, but she understands that real happiness—and not just a fragile feeling of it—is bound up with a certain kind of social world, one characterized not by treachery and dishonesty. but by trust, truthfulness, and respect.

One can of course play tricks with being (really) happy and (just) feeling happy, and certainly Fred believes that he is and does not just feel it, But those of us who know what Fred values also know that at one important level his happiness is chimerical. We know what a wretch he is, and Fred would be troubled, too, if he knew that we knew.

16

The Unhappy Immoralist

JEFFRIE G. MURPHY

All that you've just noted merely confirms my belief. . .that if we are to talk philosophy to any purpose, language must be re-made from the ground up.

—HJALMAR SÖDERBERG, *DOCTOR GLAS*

WHEN PRESENTING HIS VERSION of the ancient well-known challenge that the Sophists long ago posed to Socrates, Professor Cahn seems to be assuming at the outset—and asking us to grant—that the man he describes *is* happy. But such an assumption begs the whole question at issue here.

In both *Republic* and *Gorgias*, Plato has Socrates argue that the immoral man—even a tyrant with great power—may of course be happy as the ignorant world understands happiness but will not be happy as this concept will be truly understood by the wise philosopher.

Professor Cahn dismisses this as verbal "sleight-of-hand," but I think that such dismissal is hasty. Plato is trying to advance our philosophical understanding by making a conceptual or linguistic claim—no doubt a revisionary one—and surely not all such claims are merely useful verbal tricks. As I read Plato, he (like Philippa Foot) is suggesting that full human happiness is to be understood as the satisfaction one takes in having a personality wherein all elements required for a fully realized human life are harmoniously integrated. The immoralist lack some of these attributes—integrity, moral emotions, and the capacity for true friendship, for example. Given what he lacks, it can be granted that he may indeed be happy in some limited way—e.g., enjoying a great deal of pleasure—while insisting that he cannot be happy in the full sense.

As a matter of common language, of course, many people do not use the word "happiness" in this rich sense but tend to mean by it something like "has a whole lot of fun." Because of this, the Greek word *eudaemonia,* which in the past was generally translated as "happiness," is now often rendered as "flourishing" to avoid confusion. But some are not so quick to give up the older and deeper usage:

> [Realizing how little the clergyman cared about his wife's health or even his own] I began to think that Markel and his Cyrenäics are right: people care nothing for happiness, they look only for pleasure. They seek pleasure even flat in the face of their own happiness.[1]

Some of the spirit of Plato and Socrates is to be found in Kierkegaard's *Purity of Heart Is to Will One Thing*—where he seeks to expose the conflicts and deficiencies present in the "double-minded" person who does not organize his life around the moral good, a person whom Kierkegaard regards as self-deceived if he thinks of himself as truly happy. Kierkegaard argues for this with a blending of conceptual and psychological claims—claims about the nature of those desires he calls "temporal." The person who wills only in pursuit of temporal rather than eternal (i.e., ethico-religious)

---

1. Hjalmar Söderberg, *Doctor Glas* (New York: Anchor, 2002), 111–112.

desires will, Kierkegaard maintains, ultimately fall into boredom and despair, since the objects of these desires are vulnerable to the vicissitudes of fate and fortune and carry only temporary satisfaction. The apparent happiness of the person in bondage to temporal desires will be momentary and will mask what is in fact that person's desperate attempt to generate and satisfy new desires as the old ones become boring or their objects pass away. Kierkegaard, in *Either/Or*, calls this boredom avoidance strategy "the rotation of crops." The person who lives solely for temporal values will, according to Kierkegaard, remain in his deficient state unless he experiences and listens to the moral emotions of regret and remorse—those "emissaries from eternity" that call us to our full humanity.

Is Professor Cahn's "happy immoralist" captured by Kierkegaard's diagnosis? I think that he is. He does, after all, "relish praise," "bask in renown," and smugly "revel in his exalted position." This suggests that, like the tyrant discussed by Plato, he is attached to temporal values that are *vulnerable*—e.g., dependent on the responses of others. Since these are ultimately out of his control, must he not consciously feel or repress *fear*—a fear that may not be compatible with happiness? Professor Cahn admits that there may be a future time when his immoralist becomes unhappy, and I am inclined to think that the immoralist's conscious or repressed realization of this possibility would at the very least pose a serious obstacle to his being fully happy now. And is happiness simply a matter of *now* anyway? Perhaps, as Aristotle sometimes suggests, happiness is better understood as an attribute, not of a present moment of one's life, but of a whole life—the wisdom in the ancient Greek saying that we should call no man happy until he is dead. Finally, if there is any truth in the idea that love and friendship are among the constituents of the happiest of human lives, must not the immoralist's nature—his inability to make and honor binding commitments—forever foreclose these goods to him?

There is no doubt that Plato's and Kierkegaard's understanding of happiness does not capture everyone's understanding of the concept, and thus it must be admitted that some conceptual

The Unhappy Immoralist

or linguistic revision is going on here—just as Socrates was engaged in such revision when he made the revolutionary suggestion (*Apology*) that a good person cannot be harmed because harm (*kakon*), when properly understood, will be understood as loss of moral integrity and not as personal pain or disgrace. And if this was "sleight-of-hand," it strikes me that our concept of morality—indeed our civilization—was enriched by it. Professor Cahn's attempt to undermine the Platonic happiness tradition with his story of "the happy immoralist" thus strikes me as no more successful than an attempt to refute Socrates's claim about a good man's insulation from harm by finding a good man and hitting him in the head with a baseball bat. Doctor Glas's friend certainly overstated the case when he said that philosophy requires that language be remade from the ground up, but it is true, I think, that conceptual or linguistic revision can sometimes enlarge and deepen our moral understanding—perhaps bringing to consciousness something that was latent all along.

To sum up: When I think of the man described by Professor Cahn, I find that I *pity* him—pity him, because, with Plato, I think that he is punished simply by being the kind of person that he is. But why would I pity him if I thought he was truly happy?

71

17

Is Fred Happy?

CHRISTOPHER W. GOWANS

PHILIPPA FOOT SPEAKS CAUTIOUSLY. The passage about happiness and human nature quoted by Steven Cahn is preceded by the words "it seems that," and it is followed by a series of questions. All this is intended to illustrate her central point "that there are some concepts that we do not understand well. . .but which are, unfortunately, essentially genuine discussions of the merits of different moral systems."

Cahn has no such reservations. "Surely Fred is happy," he says, speaking of the title character of his essay, since Fred has achieved his three aims of fame, wealth, and good reputation, even though "he has no interest whatever in friends or truth" (meaning, I gather, his own truthfulness.) This purported counterexample is perplexing in several respects. Foot's suggestion concerned happiness and human nature, but the example seems mainly to pertain to happiness and morality, as the title of Cahn's essay implies. This point aside, Cahn says little about why he is so confident that Fred is happy, and we are left to speculate about his reasons.

Is Fred Happy?

One consideration is obvious: Fred has three of the things people sometimes take to be important for happiness. Perhaps Cahn thinks fame, wealth, and good reputation are sufficient for happiness. It is more likely, however, that he thinks they are sufficient for Fred's happiness, even though they would not be sufficient for many others. Most people would say that friendship is essential to genuine happiness, but Cahn thinks it not essential to Fred's happiness. Why suppose this? A subjective view of happiness would give us a reason: If you think X, Y, and Z are sufficient for your happiness, and you have them, then you are happy (whatever X, Y, and Z may be). We know too much about self-deception concerning one's own well-being to be convinced by this, and we are not likely to agree in the face of examples where *just anything* is allowed to instantiate the variables. Cahn's example gains whatever plausibility it has by featuring some of the things that many people associate with happiness.

On the other hand, Cahn's point may not be subjectivism but the importance of diversity: Different things make different people happy. No doubt this is true, and classical theories of happiness have insufficiently recognized it. Foot's point, however, is that human nature seems to impose some limits on this diversity. Is it obvious she is wrong? Are people mistaken in thinking friendship, broadly conceived, is essential to happiness? Cahn does not consider whether Fred, while sitting alone watching himself praised on his wide-screen television, ever feels lonely. Is there nothing within him that suggests that value of sharing his life with someone? Are his parents and siblings of interest only because they join in the praise of him? There is room for great variation in valuable human relationships, but happiness without any friendship is another matter (even monastics typically live in communities). Human beings are enormously dependent on one another. None of us could survive the early stages of life, and usually the latter stages, without the love and concern of others. This suggests that friendship is rather fundamental to the well-being of human beings—that we are, so to speak, hard-wired for it. We have more reason to think this than we have to think that Fred is never lonely or would never benefit from genuine friendship.

This puts in doubt the plausibility of Cahn's example. So too does his depiction of Fred as "thoroughly dishonest," while having a "reputation for probity." Why is Cahn the only one who knows the truth about Fred (who is said to be based on persons he has known)? It is more likely that Cahn is not alone and that Fred realizes this and worries he will be exposed, bringing his fame, wealth, and reputation to an end—as indeed sometimes happens. It is reasonable to suppose that Fred is not only lonely, but anxious as well (contrary to Cahn's assurances). Since he has no friends, he has no one to whom to express this. But that does not mean he lives tranquilly, free from all anxiety.

Perhaps Fred's wealth, fame, and reputation compensate for these concerns, and on balance he is happy. But if he were a real person, perhaps he will not be. Or maybe he manages to suppress these concerns. Do we really want to say, however, that real happiness may be achieved through such psychological contortions? What Cahn's example shows, if anything, is that happiness is a complex and perplexing matter, just as Foot suggested. It does not provide us with a convincing case of a happy immoralist.

Though Cahn apparently intends to make a metaethical point, his discussion has troublesome normative overtones. How are we to relate to Fred, on Cahn's account, if he falls within our domain as son, brother, colleague, neighbor, and the like? To some extent, it seems, with indifference. After all, he is happy and needs no friends, so there is no reason to to be concerned about his well-being. But also with fear. He is treacherous and may do us harm, and there is nothing we can appeal to that would change him. But if he were involved with a real-life Fred, and we were striving to live a life of compassion and hope, surely we would have more reason to suspect he is sometimes anxious and lonely, and hence warrants our concern, than we would to treat him merely with indifference or fear. Perhaps Fred is happy in some respects, but we should be most engaged with the respects in which he is probably not.

18

Fred's Happiness

CHRISTINE VITRANO

STEVEN CAHN CLAIMS THAT an immoral person can achieve happiness. As an illustration, he presents the fictitious example of Fred, a happy immoralist. Several philosophers have objected to Cahn's view, and I shall argue against those critics.

The first problem with these objections is that they fail to reflect the common understanding of happiness. Although the ancient Greeks had a tradition of conflating happiness with morality, denying that happiness was attainable by anyone who was not virtuous, I believe the word no longer retains that meaning today. When I say that someone is happy, I am referring to her state of mind. Being happy implies nothing about the value of a person's life independent of her own perception. A person's happiness is proportional to how positively she views her life; the more favorable her impression, the happier she will be.

Happiness is best described as a mental state of the subject, not as a state of affairs occurring in the world, and the concept has no necessary material conditions. We can describe someone without contradiction as "Poor, but happy, " "Wicked, but happy," or even "Alone, but happy."

Happiness is not the primary or sole reason for action; it is merely one motivation among others. Some people act out a sense of duty, or a desire for excellence, but these concerns may have nothing to do with happiness and provide no guarantee of it.

Fred views his life positively because he is attaining those goals he deems valuable, yet all three objectors express skepticism over the value of those goods and share the view that Fred's blatant immorality precludes him from happiness. But focussing on what Fred's life lacks is irrelevant to the question whether he is happy, for if Fred is not bothered by what his life is missing, he need not be dissatisfied. That I would not be happy living your life is no reason you are not happy living it.

The connection posited by Kleinig between happiness and "a certain kind of social world" may apply to some people but not to Fred. For people who value being moral, considerations of happiness clearly will be intertwined with morality, for their satisfaction will require living up to their ethical obligations. The mistake is to assume all people share these values.

Gowans makes a similar error by assuming that Fred would benefit from genuine friendships. If I am content being alone, having more friends may not increase my happiness. Although friendships, family relationships, and children are all sources of some people's happiness, to others they can become sources of misery.

Returning to the charge that Fred's happiness is unstable, I wonder whose happiness is ever "epistemologically sound" or invulnerable to "the vicissitudes of fate and fortune." I believe Fred's happiness is no less secure than anyone else's, for our moral values provide us with little protection against many sources of misery and unhappiness. For example, we can have strong attachments to other people whose health and safety are beyond our control. Likewise, we usually value our health and careers, but no matter how virtuous we are, one or both may fail. The happiness of all people is fragile, although most of us tend not to think about our situation, clinging instead to the false belief that virtue can guard us against evils. In reality, the immoralist's happiness, like the happiness of everyone else, is vulnerable to the vicissitudes of life.

Furthermore, I wonder why Gowans assumes that Fred does not have any friends; after all, Fred is supposed to be a *successful* immoralist, not an unsuccessful one. Although he is immoral, no one else knows. On the outside, Fred appears to be kind-hearted and caring; people believe he is a virtuous person. Surely then, Fred is respected by many who consider him a good friend. What distinguishes Fred is not that he has no friends but that he doesn't care whether he has any.

The same sort of misunderstanding leads Murphy to misdiagnose Fred's situation. You may pity Fred because you frown upon his lifestyle choices; you would prefer to be a more honorable (if less popular) person. Perhaps you are also skeptical about Fred's ability to keep up the charade. You may be worried that Fred's duplicity will be exposed; you may fear the repercussions if his immorality is revealed. But why assume Fred shares your values or anxieties? You might not want happiness that results from immorality, but someone else might. Your moral objection to Fred's lifestyle is a reflection of your own values and says little about the quality of Fred's life.

Thus none of Cahn's critics presents a compelling argument that challenges Fred's happiness. Those tempted to deny it seek to keep morality and happiness closely tied, because once you recognize their independence, you open the door to the dreaded question, "Why be moral?" If you acknowledge that one's happiness can come into conflict with the duty to be moral, and you agree that it is rational to pursue one's own happiness, you are forced to acknowledge that behaving immorally could be rational.

Many moral philosophers try to avoid this conclusion by denying that morality and happiness can conflict. They presume that acknowledging reasons for action other than one's moral obligations will diminish the importance of morality, or encourage people to take their moral obligations less seriously. I believe, however, the solution to the issue is not to deny the immoralist's happiness. The philosopher's attempt to steal back the word "happiness" from

the common lexicon and supply it with a "philosophical" defini-
tion is futile; it does little to improve the prospects for morality,
and only deepens the chasm between philosophy and common
sense.

19

A Challenge to Morality

Those who find Fred hard to fathom should consider the following example inspired by the plot of Woody Allen's movie *Crimes and Misdemeanors*.

Suppose a man who is happily married and highly respected as a physician makes the mistake of embarking on an affair with an unmarried woman whom he meets while she is working as a flight attendant. When he tries to break off this relationship, she threatens to expose his adultery and thereby wreck his marriage and career.

All he has worked for his entire life is at risk. He knows that if the affair is revealed, his wife will divorce him, his children will reject him, and the members of his community will no longer support his medical practice. Instead of being the object of people's admiration, he will be viewed with scorn. In short, his life will be shattered.

As the flight attendant is about to take the steps that will destroy him, he confides in his brother, who has connections to the criminal underworld. The brother offers to help him by arranging for the flight attendant to be murdered, with minimal danger that the crime will be traced to either the physician or his brother.

PART III: HAPPINESS

Should the physician consent to the killing? Doing so is clearly immoral, but, if all goes as planned, he will avoid calamity.

The physician agrees to the murder, and when it is carried out and the police investigate, they attribute it to a drifter who eventually dies of alcoholism, and the case is closed. The physician's life goes on without further complications from the matter, and years later he is honored at a testimonial dinner where, accompanied by his loving wife and adoring children, he accepts the effusive gratitude of the community for his lifetime of service. He is a happy man, taking pride in both the affection of his family and the admiration of his patients and friends.

Even most of those who might take issue with my claim that the physician is happy would agree that he is happier than he would have been had his life been destroyed. Hence his immorality enhanced his chances for happiness.

But then the feared question arises: What persuasive reasons, if any, can be offered to demonstrate that in securing his own happiness the physician acted foolishly?

20

The Case of Richard Rich

SOME CRITICS COMPLAIN THAT Fred is fictitious and the adulterous physician merely a character in a movie. Why aren't we considering a real-life situation? So here is one.

A Man for All Seasons, Robert Bolt's 1960 play about Sir Thomas More, is based on the historical record and is usually interpreted as a defense of living and dying in accord with strict adherence to moral principle. The situation, however, is not as straightforward as often supposed.

The plot is well known. King Henry VIII's desire for a son leads him to seek a divorce from his first wife, Catherine of Aragon, in order to marry Anne Boleyn. Thomas More, previously named Lord Chancellor of England, is a devout Catholic who does not agree with the King's desire but remains silent. The King, however, demands that on pain of being judged guilty of treason, all members of his court must take an oath affirming the King's supreme power in English religious affairs. More refuses and is brought to trial, where a witness commits perjury by testifying, contrary to fact, that he heard More say that Parliament did not have authority to make the King the Head of the Church. As a result, More is sentenced to death.

Such is what most remember about the story. Yet few pay attention to that damaging witness, whose name is Richard Rich.

He first appears as a hanger-on, beseeching More for a place at court, but More refuses, urging Rich to pursue a career as a teacher. Rich, however, seeks a more influential position. When he is approached by Thomas Cromwell, Secretary to Cardinal Wolsey, who wants information about More, Rich provides that help, and in exchange Cromwell arranges for Rich to become Collector of Revenues for York.

At More's trial for treason, Richard Cranmer, the Archbishop of Canterbury, administers the oath to Rich, who swears that the evidence he gives will be truthful. Rich then tells the lie that dooms More. As Rich leaves court, More notices that Rich is wearing the chain of office as Attorney General for Wales, the position he has been given in exchange for his perjured testimony. More remarks to Rich, "For Wales? Why, Richard, it profits a man nothing to give his soul for the whole world. But for Wales!"

In the 1995 movie version of the play, directed by Fred Zinnemann and starring Paul Scofield as Sir Thomas More, the action ends with More's execution, but the audience is then informed of subsequent developments. Eventually Cromwell was beheaded for high treason and Cranmer was burned at the stake. Finally— and here is the shocker— "Richard Rich became Chancellor of England and died in his bed." On that note the movie ends.

In fact, throughout his life Rich was a remarkably treacherous individual.[1] For example, he trapped Bishop John Fisher, the Chancellor of Cambridge University, into revealing that he did not accept the King as supreme head of the Church, thus leading to Fisher's trial and beheading. Later Rich participated in a plot against the King's sixth wife, Katherine Parr, that involved his personally torturing the English writer and Protestant martyr Anne Askew. Rich even provided damaging testimony against his former patron Cromwell, who then was executed. The historian Hugh

---

1. The following information is found in the entry devoted to Rich in the *Oxford Dictionary of National Biography* (Oxford: Oxford University Press, 2004).

Trevor-Roper concludes that the "dreadful Rich" is an individual "of whom nobody has ever spoken a good word."[2]

Yet Rich's career turned out to be remarkably successful. First consider his full title: Sir Richard Rich. He also acquired extensive wealth and property, became Speaker of the House of Commons and later Lord Chancellor of England. He remained active in court until his death from natural causes at about age 70. Finally, he had many children, and the line of nobility he established continued for over two centuries.

Ironically, More's taunt to Rich: "For Wales?" might have been answered: "Not merely for Wales but to acquire wealth, achieve fame, and become Lord Chancellor of England."

A Man for All Seasons is obviously a defense of the moral life. Yet it also portrays how someone who is immoral may nevertheless achieve success. In that sense it accords with the view of the ethical theorist Bernard Gert, who wrote that "a person does not need to be moral in order to be happy or live a fulfilling life."[3]

Many philosophers, past and present, have been loath to admit the possibility of a happy immoralist. They regard the concept as a threat to morality, because the greater the divergence between morality and happiness, the greater the loss of motivation to choose the moral path.

Thus they are inclined to dismiss as unrealistic any supposed examples in which by doing wrong we serve our long-term ends. I urge those inclined to take that position to consider the case of Richard Rich.

2. "Foreword," Hugh Trevor-Roper, *Lisle Letters*, ed. Muriel St. Clare Berne (Chicago: The University of Chicago Press, 1981), xiii, xviii.

3. Bernard Gert, "Comments on Cahn's "The Happy Immoralist," *Journal of Social Philosophy*, XXXV: 1, 2004, 19.

PART IV

LITERARY INSPIRATIONS

Introduction

LITERARY WORKS OFTEN STIMULATE philosophical reflection. Such is the case with the five examples that follow.

A Clockwork Orange is a novel published in 1962 by English writer Anthony Burgess. It provided the basis for Stanley Kubrick's 1971 film of the same name. Special thanks to my brother, Victor L. Cahn, for his assistance with the writing of this essay.

If Not Higher is a Yiddish tale authored by the eminent Polish writer I. L. Peretz. The notes are my own.

The Wife of Lear raises a rarely asked question about Shakespeare's immortal play *King Lear.*

Knoxville, Summer of 1915 is a short prose work written in 1938 by the American writer James Agee and set to music for voice and orchestra in 1947 by the American composer Samuel Barber.

The story of Joseph is told in chapters 37–50 of the Book of Genesis, and his death is reported at the beginning of the Book of Exodus.

21

A Clockwork Orange: On Free Will

A CLOCKWORK ORANGE HAS been the subject of much critical interpretation, but two views of the movie dominate. One proposes that director Stanley Kubrick is condemning the violence in our society, while the other suggests that he is glorifying it. To my mind, however, neither interpretation is correct, for *A Clockwork Orange* is not a film of social commentary but instead one of philosophical speculation. In attempting to raise issues about the human condition, Kubrick has simply used violence as an example of a human phenomenon. He has also used sex and music, and those who concentrate on the brutal aspects of the film are criticizing Kubrick's example, ignoring or perhaps missing that it is just that: an example. He has focused on violence because it is powerful and universal, but why it is so is not his concern. Instead, he is focused on the nature of all human action, regardless of its attractiveness.

When we first meet the central character, Alex, he is, although strangely charming, vicious and brutal, clearly not to be admired. Equally obvious, however, his later state of conditioned non-violence is portrayed as more undesirable. He may be a "true Christian," who will be allowed to go "free," as the government minister insists, but, as the prison chaplain claims, Alex is obviously not free, because he has not accepted "Christian" values through choice. Thus the implication of the film seems to be that a free human being, no matter how destructive, is preferable to a pacified individual, completely conditioned and unable to act freely.

But is Alex, who says at the end of the film, "I am cured," as free as he believes? Is he indeed unconditioned? Or has he not exchanged a more obvious, more efficient conditioning for a less obvious, less efficient form? Has the world that brought him up not at the same time conditioned him? Do not Alex's parents and friends lead him to brutality by responding only when he bullies them? Does not society condition him by reinforcing his sexual fantasies with erotic art? And what about the prison chaplain who pleads for freedom of choice? Does he not attempt to condition Alex and other listeners by trying to impose a fear of suffering in an afterlife? Perhaps, then, the film is condemning modern society by presenting a member who has responded fully to certain aspects of the conditioning process.

But an irony runs throughout the film that undercuts any social commentary. For instance, the many brutal and shocking scenes are all intruded upon humorously by such devices as incongruous background music, altered camera speeds, or an almost choreographed direction. Somehow the violence is rendered meaningless, as though the actions are neither good nor evil, but simply unreasoned, animalistic responses. Indeed, on reflection, almost all human actions in the film are cold, reflex behavior. Qualities such as sensitivity and sympathy, *human* qualities, are notably absent.

By presenting human action in such an inhuman light, by dwelling so heavily on the conditioning process, and by his emphasis on the meaning of the word *free,* Kubrick indicates that he is offering a dramatization of behaviorism. The film is a portrait of human life as a series of acquired, automatic responses to the stimuli of the environment. Like the famed Pavlov dogs, Alex learns responses that satisfy his needs, and he performs them again and again. For instance, with his parents he acts as their conditioning has taught him to react: bullying and lying. They are among the thousands of stimuli in his environment, including his friends, rival gangs, women, Beethoven's music, and the prison chaplain. Toward each Alex reacts as he has been conditioned, and that reaction replaces thinking and free choice. Kubrick implies that the Ludovico conditioning technique is merely a concentrated version of what goes on every minute of every human being's life. Alex's abhorrence of violence at the end of two weeks is not reasoned, but simply a reflex, like his attitude toward his parents. This new reaction is sharper only because it has been more efficiently conditioned. Just as Alex is not free when he leaves the Ludovico Institute, so, Kubrick suggests, no human beings are ever free. The implication is that conditioning, whether good or evil, prevents our being free. Yet conditioning is inescapable. This view has been promulgated in a sophisticated version by B. F. Skinner.[1] Granted, we recoil when we ponder the possibility that our society is conditioning violence. Perhaps more frightening, however, is the possibility that regardless of which values our society conditions, human beings can never be free agents.

This theory is highly controversial, and I have assessed it elsewhere.[2] What I am arguing here, though, is that *A Clockwork Orange* is not essentially a vision of a new world of the future, or a commentary on muggings in the subway, the violence of pro football, or the horrors of war. Rather, the movie is a dramatization of the view that human beings are mistaken if they assume that they have free will.

---

1. See, for example, B. F. Skinner, *Beyond Freedom and Dignity* (New York: Knopf, 1971).

2. See "Determinism and Freedom" in *A Philosopher's Journey: Essays from Six Decades*, the second volume of this trilogy.

22

If Not Higher: On Religion Without God

STEVEN M. CAHN

MANY SUPPOSE THAT A religious life necessarily involves believing in God, doing what is right in order to serve God, and hoping thereby to attain the bliss supposedly found in heaven. I propose instead that someone may lead a religious life without believing in God but by doing what is right in response to the needs of others and thereby potentially achieving the satisfaction that can be found on earth.

For illustration I turn to a tale by I. L. Peretz, who was described by one notable critic as "arguably the most important figure in the development of modern Jewish culture."[1] To summarize the story would fail to do it justice, and so I present it in its entirety.

❖ ❖ ❖

---

1. The *I. L. Peretz Reader*, ed. Ruth R. Wisse (New Haven and London: Yale University Press, 2002), xiii.

If Not Higher

Early every Friday morning, at the time of the Penitential Prayers,[2] the rabbi of Nemirov[3] would vanish.

He was nowhere to be seen—neither in the synagogue nor in the two Houses of Study nor at a minyan.[4] And he was certainly not at home. His door stood open; whoever wished could go in and out; no one would steal from the rabbi. But not a living creature was within.

Where could the rabbi be? Where should he be? In heaven, no doubt. A rabbi has plenty of business to take care of just before the Days of Awe.[5] Jews, God bless them, need livelihood, peace, health, and good matches. They want to be pious and good, but our sins are so great, and Satan of the thousand eyes watches the whole earth from one end to the other. What he sees, he reports; he denounces, informs. Who can help us if not the rabbi!

That's what the people thought.

But once a Litvak[6] came, and he laughed. You know the Litvaks. They think little of the Holy Books but stuff themselves with Talmud[7] and law. So this Litvak points to a passage in the *Gemarah*—it sticks in your eyes—where it is written that even Moses, our Teacher, did not ascend to heaven during his lifetime but remained suspended two and a half feet below. Go argue with a Litvak!

So where can the rabbi be?

2. A type of liturgical poetry requesting forgiveness from sins.

3. A Ukrainian city with a flourishing Jewish community in the seventeenth century but the scene of a ghastly massacre of the Jews by the Cossacks in 1648.

4. A group of ten male adult Jews, the minimum required for a communal prayer.

5. The ten-day period from Rosh Hashonah, the Jewish New Year, to Yom Kippur, the Day of Atonement.

6. A Jew from Lithuania.

7. The multi-volume compilation of Jewish law and commentary, containing the Mishnah, the core of the Oral Law, and the Gemara, a supplement to the Mishnah.

"That's not my business," said the Litvak, shrugging. Yet all the while—what a Litvak can do!—he is scheming to find out.

That same night, right after the evening prayers, the Litvak steals into the rabbi's room, slides under the rabbi's bed, and waits. He'll watch all night and discover where the rabbi vanishes and what he does during the Penitential Prayers.

Someone else might have got drowsy and fallen asleep, but a Litvak is never at a loss; he recites a whole tractate of the Talmud by heart.

At dawn he hears the call to prayers.

The rabbi has already been awake for a long time. The Litvak has heard him groaning for a whole hour.

Whoever has heard the Rabbi of Nemirov groan knows how much sorrow for all Israel, how much suffering, lies in each groan. A man's heart might break, hearing it. But a Litvak is made of iron; he listens and remains where he is. The rabbi—long life to him— lies on the bed, and the Litvak under the bed.

The Litvak hears the beds in the house begin to creak; he hears people jumping out of their beds, mumbling a few Jewish words, pouring water on their fingernails, banging doors. Everyone has left. It is again quiet and dark; a bit of light from the moon shines through the shutters.

(Afterward the Litvak admitted that when he found himself alone with the rabbi a great fear took hold of him. Goose pimples spread across his skin, and the roots of his earlocks pricked him like needles. A trifle: to be alone with the rabbi at the time of the Penitential Prayers! But a Litvak is stubborn. So he quivered like a fish in water and remained where he was.)

Finally the rabbi—long life to him—arises. First, he does what befits a Jew.[8] Then he goes to the clothes closet and takes out a bundle of peasant clothes: linen trousers, high boots, a coat, a big felt hat, and a long wide leather belt studded with brass nails. The rabbi gets dressed. From his coat pocket dangles the end of a heavy peasant rope.

The rabbi goes out, and the Litvak follows him.

8. Morning prayers.

On the way the rabbi stops in the kitchen, bends down, takes an ax from under the bed, puts it into his belt, and leaves the house. The Litvak trembles but continues to follow.

The hushed dread of the Days of Awe hangs over the dark streets. Every once in a while a cry rises from some *minyan* reciting the Penitential Prayers, or from a sickbed. The rabbi hugs the sides of the streets, keeping to the shade of the houses. He glides from house to house, and the Litvak after him. The Litvak hears the sound of his heartbeats mingling with the sound of the rabbi's heavy steps. But he keeps on going and follows the rabbi to the outskirts of the town.

A small wood stands just outside the town.

The rabbi, long life to him, enters the wood. He takes thirty or forty steps and stops by a small tree. The Litvak, overcome with amazement, watches the rabbi take the ax out of his belt and strike the tree. He hears the tree creak and fall. The rabbi chops the tree into logs and the logs into sticks. The he makes a bundle of the wood and ties it with the rope in his pocket. He puts the bundle of wood on his back, shoves the ax back into his belt, and returns to the town.

He stops at a back street beside a small, broken-down shack and knocks at the window.

"Who is there?" asks a frightened voice. The Litvak recognizes it as the voice of a sick Jewish woman.

"I," answers the rabbi in the accent of a peasant.

"Who is I?"

"Again the rabbi answers in Russian, "Vassil."

"Who is Vassil, and what do you want?"

"I have wood to sell, very cheap.." And not waiting for the woman's reply, he goes into the house.

The Litvak steals in after him. In the gray light of early morning he sees a poor room with broken, miserable furnishings. A sick woman, wrapped in rags, lies on the bed. She complains bitterly. "Buy? How can I buy? Where will a poor widow get money?"

"I'll lend it to you," answers the supposed Vassil. "It's only six cents."

"And how will I ever pay you back?" asks the poor woman, groaning.

"Foolish one," says the rabbi, reproachfully. "See, you are a poor, sick Jew, and I am ready to trust you with a little wood. I am sure you'll pay. While you, you have such a great and mighty God and you don't trust him for six cents."

"And who will kindle the fire?" asks the widow. "Have I the strength to get up? My son is at work."

"I'll kindle the fire," answers the rabbi.

As the rabbi put the wood into the oven he recited, in a groan, the first portion of the Penitential Prayers.

As he kindled the fire and the wood burned brightly, he recited, a bit more joyously, the second portion of the Penitential Prayers. When the fire was set he recited the third portion, and then he shut the stove.

The Litvak who saw all this became a disciple of the rabbi.

And ever after, when another disciple tells how the Rabbi of Nemirov ascends to heaven at the time of the Penitential Prayers, the Litvak does not laugh, He only adds quietly, "If not higher."

❖ ❖ ❖

Those last three words embody an unusual view of the relationship between God and religion. If the Litvak believed in God and God's heaven, the Litvak could conceive nothing higher. His comment thus signifies a skeptical attitude toward traditional theism. Yet he becomes a follower of the rabbi because of admiration for the rabbi's ethical commitments and the extraordinary manner in which he fulfills them.

The rabbi is not without guile. He acts surreptitiously, dons a disguise, and speaks misleadingly to the distressed woman. The deceptions, however, serve a moral purpose, and in striving to do good the rabbi is not bound by ordinary conventions. He does not slavishly follow the law but seeks to embody its spirit.

The rabbi thereby captures the essence of a religion that can be embraced even by those who do not adopt orthodox theistic beliefs. It has its rituals and prayers, but these are valuable only insofar as they accompany noble deeds. Whether to affirm the existence of God or Satan is a metaphysical question about which the rabbi and the Litvak may differ. (Who knows what the cunning rabbi believes?) The rabbi's eminence, though, rests not on the profundity of his theology but on the deep concern he shows for the sick and the poor. His wondrous actions lead the Litvak to be in awe of the rabbi's holiness.

Believing in God, the divine will, and the promise of eternal life are important aspects of many religions, but not all. The Litvak is a doubter but becomes a disciple. He laughs at the Bible but eventually reveres the rabbi. The Litvak scoffs at talk of heaven, but as events unfold his understanding grows. In the end the Litvak realizes that without ever leaving this world the rabbi in his wisdom has found a way to deal with suffering and has attained a blessedness that lies beyond any celestial vision of which human beings may dream.[9]

9. For further discussion of the concept of religion without supernaturalism, see "Religion without God" in *A Philosopher's Journey: Essays from Six Decades,* the second volume of this trilogy.

23

The Wife of Lear: On the Nature of Evil

THE DRAMATIC PERSONAE IN that summit of tragic literature, *King Lear*, includes Lear, King of Britain, and his three daughters—but not his wife. Do we ever learn anything about her, or does she remain a cipher?

The sole reference to her occurs in Act II, scene iv, when Lear, speaking to Regan, refers to "thy mother's tomb." Thus we know that Lear's wife, the Queen of Britain and the "lawful" (IV, vi) mother of Goneril, Regan, and Cordelia, has died.

Yet have we any clue to the sort of person she was? We do if we make one ordinary assumption: that the personality of children reflects the personality of at least one of their parents. Such is the case with Cordelia and Lear. Both are proud, stubborn, and capable of fidelity and love. Indeed, their very likeness leads them into conflict at the beginning of the play and reconciliation at the end.

Goneril and Regan, however, have nothing in common with their father. These daughters are capable of treachery and cruelty that lie beyond his comprehension. Who was the model for their malevolence? The obvious answer is: their mother.

How did Cordelia escape her mother's baneful influence? Remember that, as the play opens, Cordelia is quite young, not yet married, while the wife of Lear, no longer discussed, has presumably been dead many years. Hence of all three daughters, Cordelia knew her mother for the least time, perhaps hardly at all. Unlike her sisters, Cordelia was raised under the primary guidance not of her mother but of her father. Thus their affinity.

But by what means could an iniquitous woman have persuaded Lear to make her his Queen? We can almost hear her beguiling him with the same deceits later mimicked by her perfidious daughters:

> Sir, I love you more than word can wield the matter;
> Dearer than eyesight, space, and liberty;
> Beyond what can be valued, rich or rare;
> No less than life, with grace, health, beauty, honor; (I, i)

We are all prone to repeat our mistakes. So was Lear. The evidence suggests that just as at that terrible moment he was led toward his own destruction by the false flattery of Goneril and Regan, their hypocritical words echoed those uttered many years before, when the powerful yet gullible King had been duped by the wiles of another woman.

24

Knoxville, Summer of 1915: On the Good Life

WHAT IS THE ESSENCE of a good life? Contemporary philosophers have offered a variety of answers, including Susan Wolf's "actively engaging in projects of worth,"[1] Richard Kraut's "the exercise of cognitive, affective, sensory and social powers,"[2] and Stephen Darwall's "significant engagement in activities through which we come into appreciative rapport with agent-neutral values"[3] The implication appears to be that regardless of whether the goal is described as "achieving well-being," "living well," or "attaining meaning," merely following the routines of daily life is insufficient.

I want to suggest, however, that seemingly ordinary lives can be successful. The point is movingly captured in James Agee's remarkable prose poem "Knoxville, Summer of 1915."[4] The title calls to mind an unremarkable time and place at which unexceptional people carried out common activities. Yet their significance is

1. Susan Wolf, *Meaning in Life and Why It Matters* (Princeton: Princeton University Press, 2010), 26.

2. Richard Kraut, *What Is Good And Why: The Ethics of Well-Being* (Cambridge. MA: Harvard University Press, 2007), 137.

3. Stephen Darwall, *Welfare and Rational Care* (Princeton and Oxford: Princeton University Press, 2002), 75.

4. James Agee, *A Death on the Family* (New York: Penguin Books, 1957), 3–7.

illuminated by Agee's writing, which I shall take the liberty of quoting at some length.

We are talking now of summer evenings in Knoxville, Tennessee, in the time that I lived there so successfully disguised to myself as a child. It was a little bit mixed sort of block, fairly solidly lower middle class, with one or two just apiece on either side of that. The houses corresponded: middle-sized gracefully fretted wood houses built in the late nineties and early nineteen hundreds, with small front and side and more spacious back yards, and trees in the yards, and porches.. . .The men were mostly small businessmen, one or two very modestly executives, one or two worked with their hands, most of them clerical, and most of them between thirty and forty-five.

But it is of these evenings, I speak.

Supper was at six and was over by half past. . ..The children ran out first hell bent and yelling those names by which they were known; then the fathers sank out leisurely in crossed suspenders, their collars removed and their necks looking tall and shy. . ..When [the mothers] came out they had taken off their aprons and their skirts were dampened and they sat in rockers on their porches quietly.

In the evening the fathers hosed their lawns. Agree writes: *"[T]he hoses were set much alike, in a compromise between distance and tenderness of spray (and quite surely a sense of art behind this compromise, and a quiet deep joy, too real to recognize itself). . ."* The people are *"gentle happy and peaceful, tasting the mean goodness of their living. . .."* The scene is dominated by the sounds and sights of summer nights, including the hiss of the hoses and the noise of the locusts and crickets.

On the rough wet grass of the back yard my father and mother have spread quilts. We all lie there, my mother, my father, my uncle, my aunt, and I too am lying there,,,,They are not talking much, and the talk is quiet, of nothing in particular, of nothing at all in particular, of nothing at all.

In concluding, Agee meditates, *"May god bless my people, my uncle, my aunt, my mother, my good father, oh, remember them kindly in their time of trouble; and in the hour of their taking away."* (The death of Agee's father in a car accident when Agee was five

years old is the focal event in his evocative autobiographical novel
A Death in the Family, awarded the Pulitzer Prize for Fiction in
1958.)

Agee portrays families living together in a mutually sup-
portive community, and, despite their individual problems, finding some contentment. Did they engage in "projects of worth,"
exercise "cognitive, affective, sensory, and social powers," or find
"rapport with agent-neutral values"? I do not know, and I doubt
the people themselves would even have understood the questions.

Those residents of Knoxville, Tennessee, in 1915 are for the
most part forgotten, and they, along with their hopes and concerns, have disappeared. Yet they found a calming rhythm in their
lives. How many of us can claim likewise?

25

The Joseph Saga: On the Human Condition

THE BIBLICAL ACCOUNT OF the life of Joseph is related in the final chapters of the Book of Genesis with a poignant postscript that opens the Book of Exodus. The tale has inspired numerous artistic treatments, ranging from the Andrew Lloyd Webber and Tim Rice musical *Joseph and the Amazing Technicolor Dreamcoat* to Thomas Mann's monumental novel *Joseph and His Brothers*. My focus, however, is the story's embodiment of three principles essential, I believe, to understanding the human condition: I refer to them as turnabouts, trade-offs, and transience.

The narrative begins when Jacob (or Israel) gives to his best-loved son, Joseph, an ornamental tunic. As a result, Joseph's brothers, seeing that Jacob loves Joseph best, conspire to kill him by casting him into a pit in the wilderness.

Joseph is then sold to a caravan of Ishmaelites who transport him to Egypt, where he is bought by a courtier of Pharaoh named Potiphar, who takes a liking to him. Potiphar's wife, though, urges Joseph to have sexual relations with her, and when he refuses, accuses him of attacking her. As a result, Potiphar has Joseph imprisoned.

There he correctly explains other prisoners' dreams, and when Pharaoh learns of Joseph's ability, Pharaoh sends for Joseph, who interprets Pharaoh's own dreams to mean that the next seven years in Egypt will be a time of abundance, to be followed by seven years of famine. Pleased with Joseph's plan to gather food during the first seven years, then keep it as a reserve for use during the years of famine, Pharaoh places Joseph in charge of Egypt.

In time Joseph brings his entire family there and provides them with holdings in the choicest part of the country. His descendants multiply, but eventually Joseph dies. At the opening of Exodus, we read the ominous words, "A new king arose over Egypt who did not know Joseph."[1] This ruler, finding the numerous Israelites to be a threat, enslaves them, but they eventually achieve deliverance under the leadership of Moses.

Thus the story begins positively, turns negative, then positive, then negative, then positive, then negative, and so on. Each good or bad turn leads to the reverse.

The sequence suggests that good times contain the seeds of bad times, and bad times of good. In other words, a seemingly positive development is likely to carry within it negative potential, while a seemingly negative development is apt to harbor positive possibilities. Thus few situations are as troubled or untroubled as they may at first appear.

Even expressions of love, such as Jacob's gift of a coat, may unintentionally lead to harm for the one cherished. On the other hand, sufferings, such as those inflicted on Joseph by his brothers, may result in enhanced resilience and future success.

For that reason we are well-advised to avoid overconfidence in favorable situations, while resisting hopelessness when circumstances bring us low. In short, goods and evils are rarely unmitigated.

A second principle is that when we face choices in our lives, each option is potentially favorable in certain respects but unfavorable in others.

When Joseph rejects advances from Potiphar's wife, he acts morally but is victimized by her slander. When he brings his family to Egypt, he delivers them from famine but places them in a

1. Exodus 1:8.

position where they are dependent on him for their safety. In both cases he faces trade-offs, and each possible decision offers both advantages and disadvantages.

The same is typically true in our own lives. You may prefer to reside in the tranquility of a rural environment or in the bustle of urban life, but either location offers advantages and disadvantages. You may pursue an undergraduate degree at a large university with its myriad academic and extracurricular options, or you may enroll at a liberal arts college which offers fewer programs but smaller classes and more personal attention. Similarly, you may choose a high pressure job which requires long hours but offers a high salary, or you may pursue a career that provides more leisure time but less financial compensation.

In other words, alternative courses of action should be assessed as better or worse, not as all-good or all-bad. Indeed, if you think that a choice involves no trade-offs, you probably have a surprise coming.

A third principle is that fame is ephemeral. So long as Joseph is alive, his family is protected. Once he dies, however, his influence evaporates. Nevertheless, Joseph lives long enough to delight in his great-grandchildren.

We, too, should seek satisfaction independent of power or reputation, for these depend on the judgments of others and are likely to fade over time. Contentment, however, depends only on an individual's own outlook, not on anyone else's opinion, and can be found even in such everyday activities as listening to music, gardening, or spending time with family or friends.

In sum, the story of Joseph suggests that turnabouts, trade-offs, and transience are features of the human condition. At times the thought of them may be distressing, but on occasions it may bring peace of mind. Such is life.

Sources

1. *The Philosophical Review,* vol. LXXI, no. 1, 1962.

2. *Analysis,* vol. 23, no. 1, 1962. Reprinted with permission.

3. *Analysis,* vol. 23, no. 2, 1962. Reprinted with permission.

4. *Analysis,* vol. 23, no. 2, 1962. Reprinted with permission.

5. *The Journal of Philosophy*, vol. 61, no. 10, 1964. Reprinted with permission of the journal.

6. Jack J. Cohen, *The Case for Religious Naturalism,* The Reconstructionist Press, 1958, reprinted by Wipf and Stock Publishers, 2019.

7. The Reconstructionist, XXXI, 16, 1965.

8. Steven M. Cahn, *Religion Within Reason*, Columbia University Press, 2017. Reprinted with permission of the publisher.

9. "Religion Gives Meaning to Life," *The Meaning of Life: A Reader*, Third Edition, eds. E. D. Klemke and Steven M. Cahn, Oxford University Press, 2008.

10. *Religion Within Reason.*

11. *Religion Within Reason.*

12. *Religion Within Reason*

13. "Foreword," Steven M. Cahn and Christine Vitrano, *Happiness and Goodness: Philosophical Reflections on Living Well,* Columbia University Press, 2015. Revised by the author.

Sources

Sources

14. *Journal of Social Philosophy*, vol. XXXV, no. 1, 2004. Reprinted by permission.

15. *Journal of Social Philosophy*, vol. XXXV, no. 1, 2004. Reprinted by permission.

16. *Journal of Social Philosophy*, vol. XXXV, no. 1, 2004. Reprinted by permission.

17. *Journal of Social Philosophy*, vol. XXXV, no. 1, 2004. Reprinted by permission.

18. "The Happy Immoralist," *A Teacher's Life: Essays for Steven M. Cahn*, eds. Robert B. Talisse and Maureen Eckert, Rowman & Littlefield, 2009. Reprinted by Wipf and Stock, Publishers, 2021. Revised by the author.

19. *Exploring Ethics*, Fifth Edition, ed. Steven M. Cahn, Oxford University Press, 2020. Reprinted by permission of the author.

20. APA Blog (September 11, 2020), To appear in *Think, Philosophy for everyone, A Journal of the Royal Institute of Philosophy*. Reprinted by permission of Cambridge University Press.

21. *Metaphilosophy* 5, 2, 1974.

22. *Religion Within Reason*. I. L. Peretz, "If Not Higher," trans. Marie Syrkin is from *A Treasury of Yiddish Stories* by Irving Howe and Elikezer Greenberg, editors, copyright © 1953, 1954, 1989 by Viking Press, renewed © 1981, 1982 by Irving Howe and Eliezer Greenberg. Used by permission of Viking Penguin, a division of Penguin Books (USA), Inc.

23. *The Shakespeare Newsletter.* XXXVII, 3–4, 1989. Reprinted with permission.

24. APA Blog (July 2, 2019). Reprinted with permission.

25. To appear in *Think*. Reprinted by permission of Cambridge University Press

106

Works of Steven M. Cahn

Books Authored

Fate, Logic, and Time. Yale University Press, 1967; Ridgeview Publishing Company, 1982; Wipf and Stock Publishers, 2004.

A New Introduction to Philosophy. Harper & Row, 1971; University Press of America, 1986; Wipf and Stock Publishers, 2004.

The Eclipse of Excellence: A Critique of American Higher Education. Foreword by Charles Frankel. Public Affairs Press, 1973; Wipf and Stock Publishers, 2004.

Education and the Democratic Ideal. Nelson-Hall Company, 1979; Wipf and Stock Publishers, 2004.

Saints and Scamps: Ethics in Academia. Foreword by Thomas H. Powell. Rowman & Littlefield, 1986; Revised Edition, 1994; 25th Anniversary Edition, 2011.

Philosophical Explorations: Freedom, God, and Goodness. Prometheus Books, 1989.

Puzzles & Perplexities: Collected Essays. Rowman & Littlefield, 2002; Second Edition, Lexington Books, 2007.

God, Reason, and Religion. Thomson/Wadsworth, 2006.

From Student to Scholar: A Candid Guide to Becoming a Professor. Foreword by Catharine R. Stimpson. Columbia University Press, 2008.

Polishing Your Prose: How to Turn First Drafts Into Finished Work (with Victor L. Cahn). Foreword by Mary Ann Caws. Columbia University Press, 2013.

Happiness and Goodness: Philosophical Reflections on Living Well (with Christine Vitrano). Foreword by Robert B. Talisse. Columbia University Press, 2015.

Religion Within Reason. Columbia University Press, 2017.

Teaching Philosophy: A Guide. Routledge, 2018.

Inside Academia: Professors, Politics, and Policies. Rutgers University Press, 2019.

The Road Traveled and Other Essays. Wipf and Stock Publishers, 2019.

Philosophical Adventures. Broadview Press, 2020.

A Philosopher's Journey: Essays from Six Decades. Wipf and Stock Publishers, 2020.
Navigating Academic Life: How the System Works. Routledge, 2021.
Philosophical Debates. Wipf and Stock Publishers, 2021.

Books Edited

Philosophy of Art and Aesthetics: From Plato to Wittgenstein (with Frank A. Tillman). Harper & Row, 1969.
The Philosophical Foundations of Education. Harper & Row, 1970.
Philosophy of Religion. Harper & Row, 1970.
Classics of Western Philosophy. Hackett Publishing Company, 1977; Second Edition, 1985; Third Edition, 1990; Fourth Edition, 1995; Fifth Edition, 1999; Sixth Edition, 2003; Seventh Edition, 2007; Eighth Edition, 2012.
New Studies in the Philosophy of John Dewey. University Press of New England, 1977.
Scholars Who Teach: The Art of College Teaching. Nelson-Hall Company, 1978; Wipf and Stock Publishers, 2004.
Contemporary Philosophy of Religion (with David Shatz). Oxford University Press, 1982.
Reason at Work: Introductory Readings in Philosophy (with Patricia Kitcher and George Sher). Harcourt Brace Jovanovich, 1984; Second Edition, 1990; Third Edition (also with Peter J. Markie), 1995.
Morality, Responsibility, and the University: Studies in Academic Ethics. Temple University Press, 1990.
Affirmative Action and the University: A Philosophical Inquiry. Temple University Press, 1993.
Twentieth-Century Ethical Theory (with Joram G. Haber). Prentice Hall, 1995.
The Affirmative Action Debate. Routledge, 1995. Second Edition, 2002.
Classics of Modern Political Theory: Machiavelli to Mill. Oxford University Press, 1997.
Classic and Contemporary Readings in the Philosophy of Education. McGraw Hill, 1997; Second Edition, Oxford University Press, 2012.
Ethics: History, Theory, and Contemporary Issues (with Peter Markie). Oxford University Press, 1998; Second Edition, 2002; Third Edition, 2006; Fourth Edition, 2009; Fifth Edition, 2012; Sixth Edition, 2015; Seventh Edition, 2020.
Exploring Philosophy: An Introductory Anthology. Oxford University Press, 2000; Second Edition, 2005; Third Edition, 2009; Fourth Edition, 2012; Fifth Edition, 2015; Sixth Edition, 2018; Seventh Edition, 2021.
Classics of Political and Moral Philosophy. Oxford University Press, 2002; Second Edition, 2012.
Questions About God: Today's Philosophers Ponder the Divine (with David Shatz). Oxford University Press, 2002.

Works of Steven M. Cahn

Morality and Public Policy (with Tziporah Kasachkoff). Prentice Hall, 2003.

Knowledge and Reality (with Maureen Eckert and Robert Buckley). Prentice Hall, 2003.

Philosophy for the 21st Century: A Comprehensive Reader. Oxford University Press, 2003.

Ten Essential Texts in the Philosophy of Religion. Oxford University Press, 2005.

Political Philosophy: The Essential Texts. Oxford University Press, 2005; Second Edition, 2011; Third Edition, 2015; Fourth Edition, 2022.

Philosophical Horizons: Introductory Readings (with Maureen Eckert). Thomson/Wadsworth, 2006; Second Edition, 2012.

Aesthetics: A Comprehensive Anthology (with Aaron Meskin). Blackwell, 2008; Second Edition (with Stephanie Ross and Sandra Shapshay), 2020.

Happiness: Classic and Contemporary Readings (with Christine Vitrano). Oxford University Press, 2008.

The Meaning of Life, 3rd Edition: A Reader (with E. M. Klemke). Oxford University Press, 2008; Fourth Edition, 2018.

Seven Masterpieces of Philosophy. Pearson Longman, 2008.

The Elements of Philosophy: Readings from Past and Present (with Tamar Szabó Gendler and Susanna Siegel). Oxford University Press, 2008.

Exploring Philosophy of Religion: An Introductory Anthology. Oxford University Press, 2009; Second Edition, 2016.

Exploring Ethics: An Introductory Anthology. Oxford University Press, 2009; Second Edition, 2011; Third Edition, 2014; Fourth Edition, 2017; Fifth Edition, 2020; Sixth Edition, 2022.

Philosophy of Education: The Essential Texts. Routledge, 2009.

Political Problems (with Robert B. Talisse). Prentice Hall, 2011.

Thinking About Logic: Classic Essays (with Robert B. Talisse and Scott F. Aikin). Westview Press, 2011.

Fate, Time, and Language: An Essay on Free Will by David Foster Wallace (with Maureen Eckert). Columbia University Press, 2011.

Moral Problems in Higher Education. Temple University Press, 2011; Wipf and Stock Publishers, 2021.

Political Philosophy in the Twenty-First Century (with Robert B. Talisse). Westview Press, 2013.

Portraits of American Philosophy. Rowman & Littlefield, 2013.

Reason and Religions: Philosophy Looks at the World's Religious Beliefs. Wadsworth/Cengage Learning, 2014.

Freedom and the Self: Essays on the Philosophy of David Foster Wallace (with Maureen Eckert). Columbia University Press, 2015.

The World of Philosophy. Oxford University Press, 2016; Second Edition, 2019.

Principles of Moral Philosophy: Classic and Contemporary Approaches (with Andrew T. Forcehimes). Oxford University Press, 2017.

Foundations of Moral Philosophy: Readings in Metaethics (with Andrew T. Forcehimes). Oxford University Press, 2017.

Works of Steven M. Cahn

Exploring Moral Problems: An Introductory Anthology (with Andrew T. Forcehimes). Oxford University Press, 2018.

Philosophers in the Classroom: Essays on Teaching (with Alexandra Bradner and Andrew Mills). Hackett Publishing Company, 2018.

An Annotated Kant: Groundwork for the Metaphysics of Morals. Rowman & Littlefield, 2020.

The Democracy Reader: From Classical to Contemporary Philosophy (with Andrew T. Forcehimes and Robert B. Talisse). Rowman & Littlefield, 2021.

Academic Ethics Today: Problems, Policies, and Prospects for University Life. Rowman & Littlefield, 2022.

About the Author

STEVEN M. CAHN IS Professor Emeritus of Philosophy at the City University of New York Graduate Center, where he served for nearly a decade as Provost and Vice President for Academia Affairs, then as Acting President.

He was born in Springfield, Massachusetts, in 1942, and earned his AB from Columbia College in 1963 and his PhD in philosophy from Columbia University in 1966. After performing extensively as a pianist and organist, he embarked on a professorial career that included positions at Dartmouth College, Vassar College, the University of Rochester, New York University, and the University of Vermont, where he chaired the Department of Philosophy.

He served as a program officer at the Exxon Education Foundation, as Acting Director for Humanities at The Rockefeller Foundation, and as the first Director of General Programs at the National Endowment for the Humanities. He formerly chaired the American Philosophical Association's Committee on the Teaching of Philosophy, was the Association's Delegate to the American Council of Learned Societies, and was long-time President of The John Dewey Foundation, where he initiated and brought to fruition the John Dewey Lectures, now presented at every national meeting of the American Philosophical Association.

He is the author or editor of more than sixty books. A collection of essays written in his honor, edited by two of his former doctoral students, Robert B. Talisse of Vanderbilt University and Maureen Eckert of the University of Massachusetts Dartmouth is titled *A Teacher's Life: Essays for Steven M. Cahn* (Rowman & Littlefielld, 2009; Wipf and Stock Publishers, 2021).

Index

Index

Index

humans, created in God's image, 42
Hume, David, 50

If Not Higher (Peretz), 87, 91–96
immoralist
  happy, 59–60, 62–63, 64–65,
    68, 70, 75–78, 79–80, 83
  unhappy, 68–71
Israel. *See* Joseph, saga of

Jacob (father of Joseph), 103
Jesus, 45, 47–48
Job, tests of, 33–37
Joseph, saga of (on the human
    condition), 87, 102–104
*Joseph and the Amazing Technicolor
    Dreamcoat*, 102
Joseph and His Brothers (Mann),
    102
Journal of Philosophy, 3

Kaufman, Walter, 45
Kierkegaard, Søren Aabye, 69–71
King Lear (Shakespeare), 87
Kleinig, John, 59, 76
"know-how," notion of, 25
Knoxville, Summer of 1915 (Agee),
    87, 99–101
Kraut, Richard, 99
Kubrick, Stanley, 87, 88–90

Lear, King, 87, 97–98
Lear, wife of, 87, 97–98
life
  after death, 42
  essence of good life, 99–101
  meaningful life, 43–48, 83
  without God, 43–48
linguistic reform and fatalism,
    20–22, 24–26
literary inspirations, 87
  A Clockwork Orange (on free
    will), 87, 88–90

Knoxville, Summer of 1915 (on
    the good life), 87, 99–101
  If Not Higher (on religion
    without God), 87, 91–96
  saga of Joseph, 87, 102–104
  wife of Lear (on the nature of
    evil), 87, 97–98
Lloyd Webber, Andrew, 102
loneliness and happiness, 74
love, 48, 70
Ludovico conditioning technique, 90

Machiavelli, 67
A Man for All Seasons (Bolt), 60,
    81, 83
Mann, Thomas, 102
masochists, 45
metaphors applied to God, 39–40
More, Thomas, 81, 83
moral guilt, 42
moral integrity, 71, 72
moral virtue, 59, 76–78, 83
Moriarty hypothesis, 30, 49–51, 53
Moses, 103
Murphy, Jeffrey, G., 59–60, 77

nature's order, 31
necessary condition, concept of,
    7–8, 15–16, 17–19

Parr, Katherine, 82
past. *See* time and fatalism
Peretz, I. L., 87, 91, 92–96
Pharaoh, 102–103
The Philosophical Review (Taylor), 3
Plato, 68, 69, 70–71
Pojman, Louis P., 30, 43, 49, 52
The Prince (Machiavelli), 67
Potiphar, 102–103
Proverbs, 36
Psalms, 36
Purity of Heart Is to Will One Thing
    (Kierkegaard), 69

Index

www.ingramcontent.com/pod-product-compliance
Lightning Source LLC
Chambersburg PA
CBHW071830090426
42737CB00012B/2221